A Taste of the Country

— EIGHTH EDITION —

Editor: Julie Schnittka
Art Director: Ellen Lloyd
Food Editor: Mary Beth Jung
Assistant Editor: Robert Fojut
Assistant Food Editor: Coleen Martin
Test Kitchen Assistants: Judith Scholovich, Sherry Smalley
Photography: Scott Anderson, Mike Huibregtse
©1995, Reiman Publications, L.P.
5400 S. 60th Street, Greendale WI 53129
International Standard Book Number: 0-89821-191-3
Library of Congress Number: 95-67305

Pictured on front cover. Clockwise from top left: Golden Squash Soup (recipe on page 31), Walnut Graham Torte (recipe on page 61) and Apple-Topped Chops (recipe on page 20).

Pictured on back cover. Clockwise from top left: Garden-Fresh Salad (recipe on page 34), Pecan Torte (recipe on page 60), Honey Walleye (recipe on page 14) and Sunshine Muffins (recipe on page 51).

WHEN fantastic fowl stars as the flavorful fare on your menu, the meal is certain to be a hit. Thanks to the bounty of birds and stuffings featured here, you can give traditional turkey a new twist or enliven an old chicken classic.

FAIREST FOWL. Clockwise from bottom: **Chicken Kiev**, **Currant-Glazed Cornish Hens**, **Turkey with Country Ham Stuffing** and **Roasted Chicken with Rosemary** (all recipes on page 5).

Main Dishes

With these mouth-watering beef, poultry, pork, seafood and game recipes, new and interesting main courses are right at your fingertips!

CHICKEN KIEV
Karin Erickson, Burney, California
(PICTURED AT LEFT)

- 1/4 cup butter (no substitutes), softened
- 1 tablespoon snipped fresh chives
- 1 garlic clove, minced
- 6 boneless skinless chicken breast halves
- 3/4 cup crushed cornflakes
- 2 tablespoons minced fresh parsley
- 1/2 teaspoon paprika
- 1/3 cup buttermilk

In a small bowl, mix butter, chives and garlic. Shape into a 3-in. x 2-in. rectangle. Cover and freeze until firm, about 30 minutes. Flatten each chicken breast to 1/4-in. thickness. Cut the butter mixture crosswise into six pieces; place one piece in center of each chicken breast. Fold long sides over butter; fold ends up and secure with a toothpick. Combine cornflakes, parsley and paprika. Dip the chicken into buttermilk; coat evenly with cornflake mixture. Place chicken, seam side down, in a greased 13-in. x 9-in. x 2-in. baking pan. Bake, uncovered, at 425° for 35 minutes. Remove toothpicks before serving. **Yield:** 6 servings.

TURKEY WITH COUNTRY HAM STUFFING
Bobbie Love, Kapaa, Hawaii
(PICTURED AT LEFT)

- 3 cups cubed crustless day-old white bread
- 3 cups cubed crustless day-old whole wheat bread
- 1-1/2 cups cubed fully cooked ham
- 1/2 cup butter *or* margarine
- 3 cups chopped onion
- 2 cups chopped celery
- 1-1/2 teaspoons rubbed sage
- 1-1/2 teaspoons dried thyme
- 1/2 teaspoon pepper
- 1 to 1-1/2 cups chicken broth
- 1 turkey (12 to 14 pounds)

Place bread cubes in a single layer in a 13-in. x 9-in. x 2-in. baking pan. Bake at 325° for 20-25 minutes or until golden, stirring occasionally. Place in a large bowl; set aside. In a large skillet, cook ham in butter for 5-10 minutes or until edges are crisp. Remove with a slotted spoon and place over bread cubes. In the same skillet, saute the onion, celery, sage, thyme and pepper until vegetables are tender; toss with bread and ham. Stir in enough broth to moisten. Just before baking, stuff the turkey. Skewer openings; tie drumsticks together. Place on a rack in a roasting pan. Bake at 325° for 4-1/2 to 5 hours or until the thermometer reads 185°. When the turkey begins to brown, cover lightly with a tent of aluminum foil and baste if needed. Remove all stuffing. **Yield:** 10-12 servings. **Editor's Note:** Stuffing may be baked in a greased 3-qt. covered baking dish at 325° for 70 minutes (uncover for the last 10 minutes). Stuffing yields about 10 cups.

CURRANT-GLAZED CORNISH HENS
Lori Bluml, Carroll, Iowa
(PICTURED AT LEFT)

- 1 package (6 ounces) long grain and wild rice mix
- 1 medium onion, chopped
- 8 ounces fresh mushrooms, sliced
- 1/4 cup chopped celery
- 2 tablespoons cooking oil
- 1/2 cup chopped pecans, toasted
- 2 tablespoons minced fresh parsley
- 1/4 teaspoon dried thyme
- 1/4 teaspoon dried marjoram
- 4 Cornish game hens
- 2 tablespoons butter *or* margarine, softened

CURRANT SAUCE:
- 1 tablespoon butter *or* margarine
- 1/2 cup currant jelly
- 2 tablespoons fresh lemon juice
- 1/4 cup cider vinegar
- 1 tablespoon cornstarch
- 1 teaspoon salt
- 3 whole cloves

Prepare rice according to package directions. In a large skillet, saute onion, mushrooms and celery in oil until tender. Remove from the heat; add rice, pecans, parsley, thyme and marjoram. Stuff hens; rub skin with butter. Place on a rack in a shallow baking pan. Bake, uncovered, at 350° for 30 minutes. Meanwhile, for sauce, heat butter, jelly and lemon juice in a small saucepan until butter and jelly are melted. Combine vinegar, cornstarch, salt and cloves; add to pan. Bring to a boil; boil for 2 minutes. After hens have baked for 30 minutes, baste and bake for another 30 minutes or until juices run clear. Bake extra stuffing in a greased 1-qt. covered baking dish at 350° for 30 minutes. **Yield:** 4 servings.

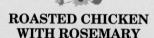

ROASTED CHICKEN WITH ROSEMARY
Isabel Zienkosky, Salt Lake City, Utah
(PICTURED AT LEFT)

- 1/2 cup butter *or* margarine
- 2 tablespoons dried rosemary
- 2 tablespoons chopped fresh parsley
- 3 garlic cloves, minced
- 1 teaspoon salt
- 1/2 teaspoon pepper
- 1 whole roasting chicken (5 to 6 pounds)
- 8 small red potatoes, halved
- 6 carrots, cut into 2-inch pieces and halved lengthwise
- 2 medium onions, quartered

In a small saucepan, melt butter. Add rosemary, parsley, garlic, salt and pepper. Place chicken on a rack in a roasting pan; tie drumsticks together. Spoon half of the butter mixture over chicken. Place the potatoes, carrots and onions around chicken. Drizzle remaining butter mixture over vegetables. Cover and bake at 350° for 1-1/2 hours, basting every 30 minutes. Uncover; bake 1 hour longer or until juices run clear, basting occasionally. **Yield:** 6 servings.

DRESSING FOR DINNER. Next time you make a ham, make dressing as you would for chicken or turkey—but without seasoning. Bake with your ham, letting the juices flavor the dressing.

5

HAM AND POTATO FRITTATA

Katie Dreibelbis, State College, Pennsylvania
(PICTURED AT RIGHT)

3 tablespoons butter *or* margarine, *divided*
1 pound red potatoes, cooked and sliced
2 cups diced fully cooked ham
1-1/2 cups thinly sliced fresh mushrooms
1 cup thinly sliced onion
1 sweet red pepper, cut into thin strips
2 teaspoons minced fresh garlic
1 tablespoon olive oil
1/2 cup minced fresh parsley *or* basil
8 eggs
Salt and pepper to taste
1-1/2 cups (6 ounces) shredded cheddar *or* Swiss cheese

In a 10-in. cast-iron or other ovenproof skillet, melt 2 tablespoons butter. Brown potatoes over medium-high heat. Remove and set aside. In the same skillet, melt the remaining butter; saute ham, mushrooms, onion, red pepper and garlic over medium-high heat until vegetables are tender. Remove and set aside. Wipe skillet clean. Heat oil over medium-low heat. Add potatoes, ham/vegetable mixture and parsley or basil. In a bowl, beat eggs, salt and pepper. Pour into skillet; cover and cook for 10-15 minutes or until eggs are nearly set. Preheat broiler; place uncovered skillet 6 in. from the heat for 2 minutes or until eggs are set. Sprinkle with the cheese and broil until melted. Cut into wedges to serve. **Yield:** 6 servings.

STUFFED COMPANY HAM

Violet Klause, Onoway, Alberta
(PICTURED AT RIGHT)

2 pounds bulk pork sausage
1 cup chopped celery
1 cup chopped onion
1 unpeeled apple, diced
3 cups soft bread crumbs
1/2 cup mincemeat
1/2 cup chopped fresh parsley
2 teaspoons dried thyme
1 fully cooked boneless ham (6 to 7 pounds)
1/2 cup apple jelly *or* honey
3 tablespoons Dijon mustard
CHUTNEY BAKED PEARS:
1 cup water
2 tablespoons lemon juice
6 ripe pears, peeled, halved and cored

1 cup chutney
1/2 cup apple juice
2 tablespoons butter *or* margarine, melted

In a skillet, brown and crumble sausage. Drain. Add the celery, onion and apple; cook over low heat, stirring occasionally, until celery is tender. Remove from heat; stir in crumbs, mincemeat, parsley and thyme. Mix well. On top of ham, cut two full-length wedges, about 1 in. wide and 3/4 in. deep, 3 in. apart. Spoon about 1/2 cup of the stuffing into each wedge. Place remaining stuffing in a greased 1-1/2-qt. covered baking dish; refrigerate. Place ham in a roasting pan and cover loosely with a foil tent. Bake at 325° for 2-1/4 hours. In a saucepan, heat jelly and mustard until jelly melts. Brush some over ham; return ham to the oven, uncovered, for 30 minutes, brushing occasionally with jelly mixture. Also place covered baking dish of stuffing in the oven at this time. For pears, mix water and lemon juice. Dip pear halves and drain. Place with cut sides up in a greased 13-in. x 9-in. x 2-in. baking pan. Mix chutney and apple juice; pour over pears. Drizzle with butter. Remove ham from oven; cover with foil and let stand 30 minutes before slicing. While continuing to bake stuffing, bake pears, uncovered, for 30 minutes, basting occasionally. **Yield:** 12-14 servings.

DILLY HAM BALLS

Dixie Terry, Marion, Illinois
(PICTURED AT RIGHT)

1 pound ground fully cooked ham
1/2 cup dry bread crumbs
1/4 cup finely chopped green onions
3 tablespoons finely chopped fresh dill *or* 3 teaspoons dried dill, *divided*
1/4 cup milk
1 egg, lightly beaten
1 teaspoon Dijon mustard
1/2 teaspoon pepper, *divided*
1 to 2 tablespoons butter *or* margarine
1 to 2 tablespoons vegetable oil
2 tablespoons all-purpose flour
1 cup water
1 cup (8 ounces) sour cream
Hot cooked noodles

In a bowl, combine ham, bread crumbs, onions, 1 tablespoon fresh dill (or 1 teaspoon dried), milk, egg, mustard and 1/4 teaspoon pepper; mix well. Shape into 1-in. balls. In a large skillet, heat 1 tablespoon butter and 1 tablespoon oil. Brown ham balls, adding remaining butter and oil as needed. Remove ham balls to a serving dish; cover and keep

warm. Pour ham drippings into a saucepan; blend in flour. Gradually add water and stir until smooth. Cook over low heat, stirring constantly until mixture thickens. Add sour cream and remaining dill and pepper; heat through, but do not boil. Pour over the ham balls. Serve over noodles. **Yield:** 6 servings.

ZESTY TURKEY

Rachel Miller, Dodge Center, Minnesota

✓ This tasty dish uses less sugar, salt and fat. Recipe includes *Diabetic Exchanges*.

2 tablespoons rubbed sage
1 tablespoon pepper
2 teaspoons curry powder
2 teaspoons garlic powder
2 teaspoons dried parsley flakes
2 teaspoons celery seed
1 teaspoon paprika
1/2 teaspoon dry mustard
1/4 teaspoon ground allspice
3 to 4 bay leaves, crumbled
1 turkey breast (4 to 4-1/2 pounds)
2 cups low-sodium chicken broth

In a small bowl, combine spices and mix well. Place turkey on a rack in a roasting pan; rub with spice mixture. Add broth to pan. Bake at 350° for 2-3 hours or until thermometer reads 170°, basting every 30 minutes. **Yield:** 6 servings. **Diabetic Exchanges:** One serving equals 3-1/2 lean meat; also, 187 calories, 85 mg sodium, 69 mg cholesterol, 3 gm carbohydrate, 32 gm protein, 4 gm fat.

Quick & Easy

TURKEY A LA KING

Mary Gaylord, Balsam Lake, Wisconsin

1 medium onion, chopped
3/4 cup sliced celery
1/4 cup diced green pepper
1/4 cup butter *or* margarine
1/4 cup all-purpose flour
1 teaspoon sugar
1-1/2 cups chicken broth
1/4 cup half-and-half cream
3 cups cubed cooked turkey *or* chicken
1 can (4 ounces) sliced mushrooms, drained
6 pastry shells *or* pieces of toast

In a skillet, saute the onion, celery and green pepper in butter until tender. Stir in flour and sugar until a paste forms. Gradually stir in broth. Bring to a boil; boil 1 minute. Reduce heat. Add cream, turkey and mushrooms; heat through. Serve either in pastry shells or over toast. **Yield:** 6 servings.

WITH its full-flavored taste, ham's always a country kitchen classic. But even this super standby needs freshening up occasionally. These delicious dishes are certain to turn humdrum ham into a newfound favorite!

AH...HAMBROSIA! Clockwise from bottom left: **Ham and Lentil Soup** (recipe on page 34), **Ham and Potato Frittata**, **Stuffed Company Ham** and **Dilly Ham Balls** (recipes on page 6).

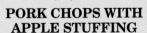

PORK CHOPS WITH APPLE STUFFING

Laura Enrico, Westford, Massachusetts
(PICTURED AT RIGHT)

1-1/3 cups soft bread crumbs
4 tablespoons butter *or* margarine
1 medium onion, finely chopped
1 celery rib, finely chopped
2 garlic cloves, minced
1 tablespoon cooking oil
1 tart apple, chopped
1 egg, beaten
1 teaspoon dried basil
1/2 teaspoon salt
1/2 teaspoon dried oregano
1/4 teaspoon pepper
8 center-cut pork chops (1/2 inch thick)
Chicken broth

In a skillet, brown bread crumbs in butter until golden; remove and set aside. In the same skillet, saute onion, celery and garlic in oil until tender. Remove from the heat. Add crumbs, apple, egg and seasonings; mix well. Lay one pork chop flat; spoon a fourth of the stuffing on top of it. Top with another chop and secure with string. Repeat with remaining chops and stuffing. Stand chops vertically but not touching in a deep roasting pan. Fill pan with 1/4 in. of chicken broth. Cover and bake at 350° for 1-1/4 hours. Uncover and bake 15 minutes longer or until chops are browned and no longer pink inside. **Yield:** 4 servings.

OLD-FASHIONED CABBAGE ROLLS

Florence Krantz, Bismarck, North Dakota
(PICTURED ON PAGE 41)

1 medium head cabbage (3 pounds)
1/2 pound ground beef
1/2 pound ground pork
1 can (15 ounces) tomato sauce, *divided*
1 small onion, chopped
1/2 cup uncooked long grain rice
1 tablespoon dried parsley flakes
1/2 teaspoon salt
1/2 teaspoon dill weed
1/8 teaspoon cayenne pepper
1 can (16 ounces) tomatoes with liquid, cut up
1/2 teaspoon sugar

Remove core from cabbage. In a large kettle or Dutch oven, cook cabbage in boiling salted water for 2-3 minutes. Remove outer leaves when softened; return to boiling water as necessary to obtain 12 leaves. Drain; remove thick center vein from leaves. In a bowl, combine beef, pork, 1/2 cup tomato sauce, onion, rice, parsley, salt, dill and cayenne pepper; mix well. Place about 1/4 cup meat mixture on each cabbage leaf. Fold in sides; starting at unfolded edge, roll up to completely enclose filling. Slice the remaining cabbage; place in a large kettle or Dutch oven. Arrange the cabbage rolls, seam side down, over cabbage. Combine tomatoes, sugar and remaining tomato sauce; pour over the rolls. Cover and bake at 350° for 1-1/2 hours. **Yield:** 6-8 servings.

DILLY CORNED BEEF AND CABBAGE

June Bridges, Franklin, Indiana
(PICTURED ON PAGE 41)

1 corned beef brisket (2-1/2 to 3-1/2 pounds)
1/4 cup honey
3 teaspoons Dijon mustard, *divided*
1 medium head cabbage (3 pounds)
2 tablespoons butter *or* margarine, melted
1 tablespoon minced fresh dill *or* 1 teaspoon dill weed

Place brisket with its seasoning packet in a Dutch oven; add enough water to cover. Cover and simmer 2-1/2 hours or until tender. Remove the brisket and place on a broiling pan; reserve cooking liquid in Dutch oven. Combine the honey and 1 teaspoon mustard; brush half over meat. Broil 4 in. from the heat for 3 minutes. Brush with the remaining honey mixture; broil 2 minutes more or until glazed. Meanwhile, cut cabbage into eight wedges; simmer in cooking liquid for 10-15 minutes or until tender. Combine butter, dill and remaining mustard; serve over the cabbage wedges and sliced corned beef. **Yield:** 6-8 servings.

DIJON CHICKEN

Carol Roberts, Dumas, Texas

1/2 cup Dijon mustard
1/2 cup water
1 broiler-fryer chicken (3 to 4 pounds), cut up
1 bag (8 ounces) herb-seasoned stuffing, crushed

In a shallow bowl, combine mustard and water; dip the chicken pieces, then roll in stuffing. Place in a greased 13-in. x 9-in. x 2-in. baking pan. Sprinkle with the remaining stuffing. Bake, uncovered, at 350° for 1 hour or until juices run clear. **Yield:** 4-6 servings.

COMPANY HAM AND NOODLES

Marjorie Schlei, Sussex, Wisconsin

1/4 cup chopped onion
2 tablespoons butter *or* margarine
10 ounces fully cooked ham, julienned (about 2 cups)
2 teaspoons all-purpose flour
1 cup (8 ounces) sour cream
1 can (8 ounces) sliced mushrooms, drained
Hot cooked noodles
Chopped fresh parsley, optional

In a skillet over medium heat, saute onion in butter until tender. Add ham; cook and stir until heated through. Sprinkle with flour and stir for 1 minute. Reduce heat to low; gradually stir in sour cream. Add the mushrooms. Cook and stir until thickened, about 2-3 minutes. Serve over noodles. Garnish with parsley if desired. **Yield:** 6 servings.

CHICKEN IN A CLOUD

JoAnn Lawer, Ishpeming, Michigan

POTATO SHELL:
3-1/2 cups hot mashed potatoes (no milk, butter or seasoning added)
1-1/2 cups (6 ounces) shredded cheddar cheese
1 can (2.8 ounces) french-fried onions
2 tablespoons chopped fresh parsley
Salt to taste
FILLING:
1-1/2 cups shredded *or* cubed cooked chicken *or* turkey
1 package (10 ounces) frozen mixed vegetables, thawed and drained
1 can (10-3/4 ounces) condensed cream of chicken soup, undiluted
1/4 cup milk
1/2 teaspoon dry mustard
1/4 teaspoon garlic powder
1/4 teaspoon pepper

Combine all of the potato shell ingredients; spread over the bottom and up the sides of a greased 2-qt. shallow baking dish. In a large bowl, combine filling ingredients; pour gently into shell. Bake, uncovered, at 375° for 40 minutes or until heated through. Let stand for 5 minutes before serving. **Yield:** 6-8 servings.

WHEN the weather starts turning cooler, set out a super spread with this warm and satisfying supper. Your family is sure to savor the harvest of colors and flavors.

AUTUMN APPEAL. Clockwise from bottom: **Pork Chops with Apple Stuffing** (recipe on page 8), **Onion Herb Bread** (recipe on page 46) and **Pumpkin Pecan Pie** (recipe on page 72).

CRANBERRY CHICKEN
Kay Simpson, Hull, Quebec
(PICTURED ABOVE)

1 broiler-fryer chicken
   (3 to 4 pounds), cut up
1/2 teaspoon salt
1/4 teaspoon pepper
2 tablespoons butter *or*
   margarine
1/2 cup diced onion
1/2 cup diced celery
1 can (16 ounces) whole-berry
   cranberry sauce
1 cup bottled barbecue sauce

Sprinkle chicken with salt and pepper; brown in a skillet in butter. Remove the chicken to a greased 13-in. x 9-in. x 2-in. baking pan. In the drippings, saute onion and celery until tender. Add cranberry sauce and barbecue sauce; mix well. Pour over chicken. Bake, uncovered, at 350° for 1-1/2 hours, basting every 15 minutes. **Yield:** 4-6 servings.

SAVORY POT ROAST
Joan Hutter, Warnick, Rhode Island
(PICTURED ON PAGE 36)

✓ This tasty dish uses less sugar, salt and fat. Recipe includes *Diabetic Exchanges*.

1 round-bone chuck roast
   (3 to 3-1/2 pounds)
1 tablespoon cooking oil
2 large onions, diced
2 garlic cloves, minced
1 can (16 ounces) tomatoes with
   liquid, cut up
1 cup water, *divided*
2 tablespoons prepared
   horseradish
1 teaspoon browning sauce

1/2 teaspoon salt, optional
1/8 teaspoon pepper
1/4 cup all-purpose flour

In a Dutch oven, brown roast in oil. Remove and set aside. In the drippings, saute onions and garlic until onions are tender. Return roast to Dutch oven. Stir in tomatoes, 1/2 cup water, horseradish, browning sauce, salt if desired and pepper. Cover and simmer for 2-3 hours or until meat is tender. Remove roast to a serving platter and keep warm. Drain all but 2 cups of pan juices. Combine flour and remaining water; stir into pan juices. Cook for 5 minutes or until thickened and bubbly. Slice roast and serve with gravy. **Yield:** 6-8 servings. **Diabetic Exchanges:** One 3-ounce serving (prepared without salt and served without gravy) equals 3 lean meat, 1 fat; also, 263 calories, 121 mg sodium, 92 mg cholesterol, 4 gm carbohydrate, 28 gm protein, 15 gm fat.

BARBECUED PORK SANDWICHES
Thelma Waggoner, Hopkinsville, Kentucky
(PICTURED ON PAGE 29)

✓ This tasty dish uses less sugar, salt and fat. Recipe includes *Diabetic Exchanges*.

1 pork shoulder roast (about 5
   pounds), trimmed and cut into 1-inch cubes
2 medium onions, coarsely
   chopped
2 tablespoons chili powder
1/2 teaspoon salt, optional
1-1/2 cups water
1 cup ketchup
1/4 cup vinegar
Hamburger rolls, split

In a Dutch oven, combine meat, onions, chili powder, salt if desired, water, ketchup and vinegar. Cover and simmer for 4 hours or until the meat falls apart easily. Skim off the excess fat. With a slotted spoon, remove meat, reserving cooking liquid. Shred the meat with two forks or a pastry blender. Return to the cooking liquid and heat through. Serve on rolls. **Yield:** 16 servings. **Diabetic Exchanges:** One serving (without added salt or a roll) equals 3 lean meat, 1 vegetable; also, 202 calories, 219 mg sodium, 84 mg cholesterol, 4 gm carbohydrate, 24 gm protein, 9 gm fat. **If Cooking for Two:** Freeze in serving-size portions to have a quick and easy meal.

ADD SPICE TO YOUR LIFE. To spice up your chicken, try adding taco seasoning or a blend of herbs to a cornmeal coating.

COBRE VALLEY CASSEROLE
Carolyn Deming, Miami, Arizona

1 pound ground beef
1 celery rib, chopped
1 medium onion, chopped
1 package (1-1/4 ounces) taco
   seasoning mix
1/4 cup water
2 cans (15 to 16 ounces *each*)
   refried beans
1 can (4 ounces) chopped
   green chilies, optional
1 cup (4 ounces) shredded
   cheddar cheese
2 green onions, sliced
1 large tomato, peeled, seeded
   and chopped
1/3 cup pitted ripe olives,
   chopped
1-1/2 cups crushed tortilla chips

In a large skillet, cook beef, celery and onion until meat is browned; drain. Stir in taco mix, water, beans and green chilies if desired; mix well. Pour into a 2-1/2-qt. baking dish. Bake, uncovered, at 350° for 30 minutes or until heated through. Top with cheese, green onions, tomato, olives and chips. **Yield:** 6-8 servings.

SAUERKRAUT STUFFING
Mary Brown, Rochester, Minnesota
(PICTURED ON PAGE 40)

3/4 cup shredded raw potatoes
3/4 cup chopped onion
1/4 cup butter *or* margarine
1 can (14 ounces) sauerkraut,
   rinsed and drained
2 tablespoons minced fresh
   parsley *or* 2 teaspoons dried
   parsley flakes
1/2 teaspoon caraway seed
1/4 teaspoon salt
1/4 teaspoon pepper
1 broiler-fryer chicken
   (3-1/2 to 4 pounds)
3/4 cup water
1/4 cup all-purpose flour

In a large skillet, saute the potatoes and onion in butter until onion is tender (potatoes will still be firm). Remove from the heat. Stir in sauerkraut, parsley and seasonings; mix well. Stuff chicken cavity; place on a rack in roasting pan. Roast, uncovered, at 375° for 2 hours or until chicken is tender and juices run clear. Remove to a serving platter and keep warm. Measure 3/4 cup of the pan drippings; pour into a saucepan. Combine water and flour; add to drippings. Cook and stir until gravy boils; boil 1 minute. Serve with the chicken. **Yield:** 4 servings.

MEATBALL SANDWICHES
Sharon Simcizen, Bozeman, Montana
(PICTURED ON PAGE 71)

SAUCE:
- 1/2 pound bulk Italian sausage
- 1/2 cup chopped onion
- 1/2 cup chopped green pepper
- 1-1/2 cups stewed tomatoes
- 2 cans (8 ounces *each*) tomato sauce
- 1 can (12 ounces) tomato paste
- 2 teaspoons brown sugar
- 1 teaspoon garlic powder
- 1/2 teaspoon dried oregano
- 1/2 teaspoon dried basil

MEATBALLS:
- 1 pound ground beef
- 1 pound bulk Italian sausage
- 2 eggs, lightly beaten
- 1/2 cup dry bread crumbs
- 3 tablespoons milk
- 1 teaspoon dried basil
- 3/4 teaspoon salt
- 1/8 teaspoon pepper
- 1/8 teaspoon dried oregano
- 1/8 teaspoon rubbed sage
- 3 tablespoons olive oil

Rolls
Sliced mozzarella cheese, optional

In a Dutch oven, cook sausage, onion and green pepper until the sausage is browned and the vegetables are tender; drain. Add the remaining sauce ingredients; bring to a boil. Cover and simmer. Meanwhile, in a bowl, combine the first 10 meatball ingredients. Shape into 1-in. balls. Brown in oil; drain. Add to the sauce; cover and simmer for 2 hours. Serve on rolls. Top with cheese if desired. **Yield:** 10-12 servings.

PORKETTES
Christy Jefferson, Reno, Nevada

- 1 pound ground fully cooked ham
- 1 egg, lightly beaten
- 1/4 cup sweet pickle relish
- 1 teaspoon prepared mustard
- 2 cups mashed cooked sweet potatoes
- 1 to 3 teaspoons grated orange peel
- 1/2 teaspoon salt
- 1/8 teaspoon pepper
- 8 bacon strips, halved lengthwise
- 1 can (20 ounces) pineapple slices, drained and halved horizontally

In a bowl, combine the ham, egg, relish and mustard. Shape 1/3 cupfuls into eight patties the same diameter as the pineapple rings. Combine the sweet potatoes, orange peel, salt and pepper.

Shape 1/4 cupfuls into eight patties the same diameter as the pineapple rings. On a lightly greased 15-in. x 10-in. x 1-in. baking sheet, assemble in the following order: Cross 2 strips of bacon, 1 pineapple slice, 1 ham patty, 1 sweet potato patty and 1 pineapple slice. Fold bacon ends up and over top; secure with a toothpick. Bake at 350° for 50-55 minutes or until bacon is crisp. Remove toothpicks; serve immediately. **Yield:** 4-6 servings.

PINEAPPLE HAM LOAF
Doris Christman, Middletown, Pennsylvania
(PICTURED ON PAGE 66)

- 2 eggs
- 1/2 cup milk
- 1 cup finely crushed saltines
- 1/4 teaspoon pepper
- 1-1/2 pounds ground fully cooked ham
- 1 pound ground fresh pork

SAUCE:
- 1 cup packed brown sugar
- 1/3 cup vinegar
- 1/4 cup water
- 1 teaspoon prepared mustard
- 1 can (8 ounces) crushed pineapple, undrained

In a large bowl, beat the eggs; add milk, crackers and pepper. Add the ham and pork; mix well. Shape into a 9-in. x 4-in. loaf and place in a shallow baking dish; insert a meat thermometer. In a small bowl, combine sauce ingredients; pour over loaf. Bake at 350° until thermometer reads 170°, about 1-1/2 hours, basting frequently. **Yield:** 6-8 servings.

BEEF 'N' CHEESE BRAID
Sharon Euliss, McLeansville, North Carolina

- 1 package (1/4 ounce) active dry yeast
- 3/4 cup warm water (110° to 115°)
- 1/4 cup butter *or* margarine, *divided*
- 2-3/4 to 3 cups all-purpose flour
- 1 tablespoon sugar
- 1/2 teaspoon salt
- 1 egg
- 1/2 cup shredded dried beef
- 1/2 cup shredded Swiss cheese
- 1-1/2 teaspoons dried basil

In a large mixing bowl, dissolve yeast in water. Soften 2 tablespoons butter; add

to yeast mixture with 1-1/2 cups flour, sugar, salt and egg; beat until smooth. Add enough remaining flour to make a soft dough. Turn out onto a floured surface; knead until smooth and elastic, about 6-8 minutes. Place in a greased bowl, turning once to grease top. Cover and let rise in a warm place until doubled, about 1 hour. Combine the beef, cheese and basil; set aside. Punch dough down. Roll into a 12-in. x 9-in. rectangle. Cut dough lengthwise into three 12-in. x 3-in. strips. Melt remaining butter; brush some over strips. Divide beef mixture in thirds and sprinkle down the center of each strip. Bring lengthwise edges together and pinch to seal, forming a rope. Place on a greased baking sheet, seam side down. Secure one end and braid the ropes together; secure other end. Cover and let rise in a warm place until doubled, about 30 minutes. Brush with remaining melted butter. Bake at 375° for 25 minutes or until golden brown. Slice and serve warm. **Yield:** 1 loaf.

SHRIMP WIGGLE
Lucille Nicholls, Hurricane, Utah

- 1 cup chopped onion
- 1/4 cup butter *or* margarine
- 3 tablespoons all-purpose flour
- 2 cups milk
- 4 ounces process American cheese, cubed
- 1 can (14-1/2 ounces) tomatoes with liquid, cut up
- 2 cans (4-1/4 ounces *each*) shrimp, rinsed and drained
- 1 cup frozen peas

Salt to taste
Chow mein noodles
Paprika

In a medium saucepan, cook onion in butter until tender. Add flour; stir until thickened and bubbly. Add milk all at once; cook and stir until thickened and bubbly. Stir in cheese until melted. Add tomatoes, stirring constantly. Add shrimp and peas; heat through. Season to taste with salt. Serve over chow mein noodles; sprinkle with paprika. **Yield:** 6 servings.

WHITE'S JUST RIGHT! If your family prefers white meat to dark meat, prepare a smaller turkey and a turkey breast; there will be plenty of white meat for everyone.

DURING THE YEAR, you're bound to open your house to friends and family. And these palate-pleasing possibilities are guaranteed to offer the best tastes of any season.

PRIME POULTRY. Clockwise from lower left: **Marinated Turkey, Roasted Duck with Apple-Raisin Dressing, Turkey with Herbed Rice Dressing, Dutch Potato Poultry Stuffing, Goose with Apple-Prune Stuffing, Sausage-Pecan Turkey Stuffing, Creole-Stuffed Turkey** and **Chicken Royale** (all recipes on pages 14 and 15).

ROASTED DUCK WITH APPLE-RAISIN DRESSING
Fran Kirchhoff, Harvard, Illinois
(PICTURED ON PAGE 12)

2 domestic ducklings
(4 to 5 pounds *each*)
Salt
DRESSING:
1 tube (12 ounces) bulk pork
sausage
1/2 cup chopped onion
1/2 cup chopped celery
1 cup chopped peeled apple
1 cup golden raisins
1/2 cup water
1-1/2 teaspoons salt
1 teaspoon rubbed sage
1/4 teaspoon pepper
2 tablespoons chopped fresh
parsley
8 cups cubed crustless day-old
white bread
3 eggs, lightly beaten
1/2 cup chicken broth

Sprinkle the inside of ducklings with salt; prick skin well all over and set aside. In a large skillet, cook sausage with onion and celery until sausage is no longer pink and vegetables are tender. Add apple and simmer for 3 minutes, stirring occasionally; drain. Meanwhile, simmer raisins in water for 8 minutes; do not drain. In a large bowl, combine sausage mixture, raisins, salt, sage, pepper and parsley; mix well. Add the bread cubes, eggs and broth; mix lightly. Divide and spoon into ducklings. Place with breast side up on a rack in a large shallow roasting pan. Bake, uncovered, at 375° for 1-3/4 to 2-1/4 hours or until the thermometer reads 185°. Drain fat from pan as it accumulates. Remove all dressing. **Yield:** 4 servings.

GOOSE WITH APPLE-PRUNE STUFFING
Violet Klause, Onoway, Alberta
(PICTURED ON PAGE 13)

1 domestic goose
(10 to 12 pounds)
Salt
STUFFING:
2 cups chopped celery
1 cup chopped onion
1 garlic clove, minced
3 tablespoons butter *or*
margarine
6 cups chopped peeled apples
1 package (12 ounces) pitted
prunes, cut up
1/3 cup chopped fresh parsley
1 tablespoon rubbed sage
1/2 teaspoon salt

1/4 teaspoon pepper
1/4 teaspoon ground thyme
1 bay leaf, crumbled
1 cup apple juice
1 egg, lightly beaten
3 to 4 cups coarse bread
crumbs
GLAZE (optional):
1 cup orange juice
1/2 cup chili sauce
2 tablespoons cornstarch
1 tablespoon brown sugar
1 tablespoon soy sauce
1 teaspoon prepared mustard
1/4 teaspoon garlic powder

Sprinkle inside of goose with salt. Prick skin well; set aside. In a skillet, saute celery, onion and garlic in butter; transfer to a large bowl. Add the next 10 ingredients. Add bread crumbs until stuffing has the desired consistency. Stuff the goose. Place with breast side up on a rack in a large shallow roasting pan. Bake, uncovered, at 350° for 3 to 3-1/2 hours or until thermometer reads 185°. Drain fat from pan as it accumulates. If desired, make glaze: Combine all ingredients in a saucepan. Cook and stir until bubbly; cook and stir 2 minutes more. Brush over the goose during the last 20 minutes of baking. Remove all stuffing. **Yield:** 8-10 servings.

MARINATED TURKEY
Wilma Lovejoy, Hastings, Nebraska
(PICTURED ON PAGE 12)

1/2 cup soy sauce
1/2 cup vegetable oil
2 tablespoons honey
2 teaspoons Worcestershire
sauce
1 teaspoon ground ginger
1 teaspoon dry mustard
1 teaspoon lemon juice
2 garlic cloves, minced
6 to 7 pounds fresh turkey
parts
1/4 cup all-purpose flour, optional
Salt and pepper, optional

In a small bowl, combine the soy sauce, oil, honey, Worcestershire sauce, ginger, mustard, lemon juice and garlic. Place turkey parts in a large plastic heavy-duty freezer bag; add marinade. Close the bag; refrigerate overnight, turning bag occasionally. Arrange turkey parts in a single layer in a large shallow roasting pan. Pour marinade over turkey. Bake, uncovered, at 325° for 1-1/2 to 2 hours or until tender. Baste occasionally if desired. Remove turkey to serving platter and keep warm. If desired, make gravy: Strain pan juices into a large measuring cup. Skim fat and reserve 1/4 cup in a medium saucepan; discard remaining fat. Blend flour into saucepan. Add water

to pan juices to make 2 cups. Add to saucepan; cook and stir until thickened and bubbly. Cook and stir 1 minute longer. Season with salt and pepper. Serve with turkey. **Yield:** 8-10 servings.

HONEY WALLEYE
Kitty McCue, St. Louis Park, Minnesota
(PICTURED ON BACK COVER)

1 egg
2 teaspoons honey
2 cups crushed butter-flavored
crackers (about 45 to 50)
1/2 teaspoon salt
4 to 6 walleye fillets
(1-1/2 to 2 pounds)
1/3 to 1/2 cup cooking oil
Lemon wedges, optional

In a shallow bowl, beat egg; add honey. In a plastic bag, combine crackers and salt. Dip fish in egg mixture, then shake in bag until coated. In a skillet, cook fillets in oil for 3-5 minutes per side or until golden and fish flakes easily with a fork. Serve with lemon wedges if desired. **Yield:** 4-6 servings.

DUTCH POTATO POULTRY STUFFING
Sarah Krout, Warrington, Pennsylvania
(PICTURED ON PAGE 13)

5 cups mashed potatoes
(without milk, butter or
seasoning)
6 cups cubed crustless day-old
white bread
2-1/2 cups chopped onion
1 cup chopped celery leaves
1 cup chopped fresh parsley
3 tablespoons butter *or*
margarine, melted
1 teaspoon salt
3/4 teaspoon pepper
3 eggs
1 tablespoon all-purpose flour
1 cup milk
1 turkey (12 to 14 pounds)

In a large bowl, combine potatoes, bread cubes, onion, celery leaves, parsley, butter, salt and pepper. In a small bowl, beat eggs and flour. Stir in milk; pour into the potato mixture and mix well. Add more milk if filling seems dry. Just before baking, stuff the turkey. Skewer openings; tie drumsticks together. Place on a rack in a roasting pan. Bake at 325° for 4-1/2 to 5 hours or until thermometer reads 185°. When turkey begins to brown, cover lightly with a tent of aluminum foil and baste if needed. Remove all stuffing. **Yield:** 10-12 servings. **Editor's Note:**

Stuffing may be baked in a greased 3-qt. covered baking dish at 325° for 70 minutes (uncover for the last 10 minutes). Stuffing yields about 10 cups.

CREOLE-STUFFED TURKEY
Sandy Szwarc, Albuquerque, New Mexico
(PICTURED ON PAGE 13)

4 cups cubed corn bread
2 cups cubed crustless day-old whole wheat bread
1 cup chopped fully cooked ham
3/4 cup chopped smoked kielbasa
1/2 cup finely diced sweet red pepper
1/2 cup finely diced green pepper
1/4 cup chopped celery
3 tablespoons finely diced onion
2-1/2 teaspoons creole seasoning*
2 eggs
1 to 1-1/2 cups chicken broth
1 turkey (8 to 10 pounds)

In a large bowl, combine the first 10 ingredients; add enough chicken broth to moisten. Just before baking, stuff the turkey. Skewer openings; tie drumsticks together. Place on a rack in a roasting pan. Bake at 325° for 3-1/2 to 4 hours or until thermometer reads 185°. When the turkey begins to brown, cover lightly with a tent of aluminum foil and baste if needed. Remove all stuffing. **Yield:** 6-8 servings. (*You may substitute the following spices instead of the creole seasoning: 1 teaspoon *each* paprika and garlic powder, and 1/4 teaspoon *each* cayenne pepper, dried thyme and ground cumin.) **Editor's Note:** Stuffing may be baked in a greased 2-qt. covered baking dish at 325° for 70 minutes (uncover during the last 10 minutes). Stuffing yields about 6 cups.

TURKEY WITH HERBED RICE DRESSING
Melanie Habener, Lompoc, California
(PICTURED ON PAGE 12)

1/2 pound bulk pork sausage
1/2 pound ground beef
1/2 cup chopped onion
2 eggs, lightly beaten
2 tablespoons chopped fresh parsley
2 tablespoons chopped celery leaves
1 tablespoon poultry seasoning
2 teaspoons salt, *divided*

2 teaspoons pepper, *divided*
3/4 teaspoon garlic powder, *divided*
4 cups cooked white rice, cooled
3 garlic cloves, minced
1 teaspoon *each* dried thyme, tarragon and marjoram
1 turkey (10 to 12 pounds)
2 cans (14-1/2 ounces *each*) chicken broth
3 tablespoons butter *or* margarine

In a large skillet, brown pork, beef and onion; drain. In a large bowl, combine eggs, parsley, celery leaves, poultry seasoning, 1 teaspoon salt, 1 teaspoon pepper and 1/2 teaspoon garlic powder; mix well. Add meat mixture and rice. Just before baking, stuff turkey. Skewer openings; tie drumsticks together. Place on a rack in a roasting pan. Combine garlic, thyme, tarragon, marjoram and remaining salt, pepper and garlic powder; rub over turkey. Add broth and butter to pan. Bake at 325° for 4 to 4-1/2 hours or until thermometer reads 185°, basting frequently. When turkey begins to brown, cover lightly with a tent of aluminum foil. Remove all dressing. **Yield:** 8-10 servings. **Editor's Note:** Dressing may be baked in a greased 2-1/2-qt. covered baking dish at 325° for 70 minutes (uncover during the last 10 minutes). Dressing yields about 8 cups.

CHICKEN ROYALE
Nancy Schubert, Lake Forest, Illinois
(PICTURED ON PAGE 13)

4 whole boneless chicken breasts
2 cups seasoned bread crumbs
2 tablespoons finely chopped onion
1/2 teaspoon salt
Pinch pepper
1/4 teaspoon poultry seasoning
10 tablespoons butter *or* margarine, melted, *divided*
1/2 cup hot water
1 tablespoon minced fresh parsley
1/2 cup all-purpose flour
1/2 teaspoon paprika
SOUR CREAM MUSHROOM SAUCE:
1/2 pound fresh mushrooms, sliced
1/4 cup chopped onion
2 tablespoons butter *or* margarine
2 tablespoons all-purpose flour
1/2 teaspoon salt
1/2 teaspoon pepper
1/2 cup heavy cream
1/2 cup sour cream

Place the chicken breasts with skin side down on a work surface; pound lightly with a meat mallet to an even thickness. For stuffing, combine the bread crumbs, onion, salt, pepper, poultry seasoning, 2 tablespoons butter, water and parsley. Place about 1/3 cup stuffing on each breast; fold in half. Secure with toothpicks. Combine flour and paprika; coat chicken. Place, skewered side down, in a greased 11-in. x 7-in. x 2-in. baking dish. Drizzle with remaining butter. Bake, uncovered, at 325° for 1-1/4 hours or until tender. Meanwhile, for sauce, saute mushrooms and onion in butter until tender. Stir in flour, salt and pepper. Gradually add heavy cream. Cook and stir until bubbly; cook and stir 1 minute more. Reduce heat; add sour cream. Stir just until heated through; do not boil. Serve over chicken. **Yield:** 4 servings.

SAUSAGE-PECAN TURKEY STUFFING
Sharon Miller, Millet, Alberta
(PICTURED ON PAGE 13)

9 cups soft bread crumbs
1 pound bulk pork sausage
2 cups chopped onion
1/4 cup butter *or* margarine
3 unpeeled tart apples, coarsely chopped
1 cup chopped pecans
1/2 cup minced fresh parsley
1-1/2 teaspoons dried thyme
1 teaspoon rubbed sage
1/4 teaspoon salt
1/4 teaspoon pepper
1/4 cup apple juice
Chicken broth
1 turkey (14 to 16 pounds)

Place bread crumbs in a large bowl. In a large skillet, cook sausage and onion in butter until sausage is no longer pink and onion is tender; do not drain. Add to bread crumbs. Stir in apples, pecans, parsley, thyme, sage, salt and pepper; stir in apple juice and enough broth to moisten. Just before baking, stuff the turkey. Skewer openings; tie drumsticks together. Place on a rack in a roasting pan. Bake at 325° for 5 to 5-1/2 hours or until the thermometer reads 185°. When the turkey begins to brown, cover lightly with a tent of aluminum foil and baste if needed. Remove all stuffing. **Yield:** 12-14 servings. **Editor's Note:** Stuffing may be baked in a greased 3-qt. covered baking dish at 325° for 70 minutes (uncover for the last 10 minutes). Stuffing yields about 12 cups.

WHEN a kitchen's a country one, chances are cabbage and sauerkraut are cooked there often. So how do you keep those old favorites fresh? These family-tested recipes are sure to bring exciting new tastes into your home.

HEADS UP! Clockwise from top: **Stuffed Whole Cabbage**, **Country Pork 'n' Sauerkraut** (recipes on page 17), **Creamed Cabbage Soup** (recipe on page 28) and **Spinach Slaw** (recipe on page 30).

COUNTRY PORK 'N' SAUERKRAUT
Donna Hellendrung, Minneapolis, Minnesota
(PICTURED AT LEFT)

2 pounds country-style pork ribs
1 medium onion, chopped
1 tablespoon cooking oil
1 can (14 ounces) sauerkraut, undrained
1 cup applesauce
2 tablespoons brown sugar
2 teaspoons caraway seed
1 teaspoon garlic powder
1/2 teaspoon pepper

In a Dutch oven, cook ribs and onion in oil until ribs are browned and onion is tender. Remove from the heat. Combine remaining ingredients and pour over ribs. Cover and bake at 350° for 1-1/2 to 2 hours or until ribs are tender. **Yield:** 4 servings.

STUFFED WHOLE CABBAGE
Wyn Jespersen, Suffield, Connecticut
(PICTURED AT LEFT)

SAUCE:
1 can (28 ounces) tomatoes with liquid, cut up
1 can (6 ounces) tomato paste
1 garlic clove, minced
1-1/2 teaspoons dried oregano
1 teaspoon dried thyme
1 teaspoon brown sugar
1/2 teaspoon salt
FILLING:
1 pound ground beef
1 medium onion, chopped
1 large head cabbage (4 pounds)
3/4 cup cooked rice
1 egg, beaten
1 teaspoon salt
1/2 teaspoon pepper
2-1/4 cups water, *divided*
3 tablespoons cornstarch
2 tablespoons shredded Parmesan cheese

Combine sauce ingredients; set aside. In a skillet, cook beef and onion until meat is browned and onion is tender; remove from the heat and drain. Leaving a 1-in. shell and the core intact, cut out and chop the inside of the cabbage. To beef, add 1 cup chopped cabbage, 1 cup sauce, rice, egg, salt and pepper; mix well. Spoon into cabbage shell. Place 2 cups water, the remaining chopped cabbage and the remaining sauce in a Dutch oven; mix well. Carefully add stuffed cabbage, meat side up. Cover and bring to a boil. Reduce

heat; cover and simmer 1-1/2 hours or until whole cabbage is tender. Remove cabbage to a serving platter and keep warm. Combine the cornstarch and remaining water; add to Dutch oven. Bring to a boil, stirring constantly; boil for 2 minutes. Pour over the cabbage; sprinkle with Parmesan cheese. Cut into wedges to serve. **Yield:** 8 servings.

HAM A LA KING
Doris Christman, Middletown, Pennsylvania
(PICTURED ON PAGE 49)

2 tablespoons butter *or* margarine
1/4 cup diced green pepper
3 tablespoons sliced green onions
1 cup sliced fresh mushrooms
1 package (10 ounces) frozen peas, cooked and drained
2 cups cubed fully cooked ham
3/4 teaspoon dry mustard
1/2 teaspoon salt
3 hard-cooked eggs, coarsely chopped
WHITE SAUCE:
1/4 cup butter *or* margarine
1/4 cup all-purpose flour
1/4 teaspoon salt
Dash white pepper
2 cups milk
1 package (10 ounces) frozen puff pastry shells, baked

In a skillet, melt butter over medium heat. Add the green pepper, onions and mushrooms; cook and stir until tender. Stir in peas, ham, mustard and salt; heat through. Gently stir in eggs; set aside. For sauce, melt the butter in a saucepan. Add flour, salt and pepper; stir to make a smooth paste. Add the milk all at once; cook and stir until thickened and bubbly. Cook and stir 1 minute more. Add ham mixture and heat through. Serve in pastry shells. **Yield:** 6 servings.

MUSHROOM ALMOND CHICKEN
Mike Talbot, Boise, Idaho

4 ounces fresh mushrooms, sliced
1 garlic clove, minced
1 tablespoon butter *or* margarine
1/2 teaspoon lemon pepper
1/4 teaspoon cayenne pepper
1 broiler-fryer chicken (3 to 3-1/2 pounds), skinned and cut up
3 eggs, lightly beaten
1/4 cup buttermilk

1/4 teaspoon salt
1-1/2 cups Italian-style bread crumbs
1/2 cup chopped almonds
1-1/2 teaspoons dried basil
1/2 teaspoon dried oregano
1 cup (4 ounces) shredded Monterey Jack cheese, optional

In a skillet, saute mushrooms and garlic in butter; set aside. Combine lemon and cayenne peppers; sprinkle over the chicken and let stand for 10 minutes. In a shallow bowl, combine eggs, buttermilk and salt. In another bowl, mix the bread crumbs, almonds, basil and oregano. Dip chicken in buttermilk mixture, then in crumb mixture, coating well. Place in a 13-in. x 9-in. x 2-in. baking pan; sprinkle with mushroom mixture. Cover and bake at 350° for 50 minutes. Uncover and bake 20 minutes longer. If desired, sprinkle with cheese and let stand for 5 minutes. **Yield:** 4 servings.

FESTIVE PORK ROAST
Karen Bridges, Plant City, Florida
(PICTURED ON PAGE 59)

1/2 cup dry cooking sherry *or* chicken broth
1/2 cup soy sauce
2 garlic cloves, minced
2 tablespoons dry mustard
2 teaspoons dried thyme
1 teaspoon ground ginger
1 boneless rolled pork loin roast (4 to 5 pounds)
APRICOT SAUCE:
1 jar (10 to 12 ounces) apricot preserves
2 tablespoons dry cooking sherry *or* chicken broth
1 tablespoon soy sauce

In a large plastic bag or glass dish, combine first six ingredients; mix well. Add pork roast, turning to coat all sides. Cover and refrigerate 3-4 hours, turning occasionally. Remove meat and discard marinade. Place roast with fat side up on a rack in a shallow roasting pan. Insert meat thermometer. Bake, uncovered, at 325° for 2 to 2-1/2 hours or until the thermometer reads 160°. Cover and let stand 15 minutes before carving. Meanwhile, in a small saucepan, combine apricot sauce ingredients. Heat and stir until well mixed and heated through. Serve with roast. **Yield:** 8-10 servings.

WHETHER you're cooking a bright-and-early breakfast, light and tasty lunch or scrumptious supper, the possible uses for ham are endless! So, go ahead, "ham it up" at your next meal by preparing one of these meaty dishes.

HAM WITH *M-M-M!* Clockwise from lower left: **Ham and Cheese Calzones**, **Sauerkraut Ham Balls**, **Ham Pasties**, **Breakfast Ham Ring**, **Festive Ham Glaze**, **Creamed Ham and Asparagus** (recipes on pages 20 and 21), **Ham Pasta Salad** (recipe on page 28) and **Cheddar Ham Chowder** (recipe on page 30).

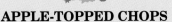

APPLE-TOPPED CHOPS
Susan Vinson, Granite Falls, North Carolina
(PICTURED ON FRONT COVER)

6 pork chops (3/4 to 1 inch thick)
1 tablespoon cooking oil
1 medium onion, thinly sliced into rings
1/2 cup raisins, *divided*
3 medium apples, cut into 1/2-inch slices
1 cup apple juice
1 tablespoon brown sugar
1 teaspoon salt
1/2 teaspoon dried basil, crushed
1/4 teaspoon ground nutmeg
1/8 teaspoon ground cloves

In a large skillet, brown pork chops in oil over medium heat. Place in an ungreased 3-qt. baking dish. Place onion rings over the chops. Sprinkle with two-thirds of the raisins. Arrange the apple slices on top and sprinkle with remaining raisins. Combine the apple juice, brown sugar, salt, basil, nutmeg and cloves; pour over all. Cover and bake at 350° for 1 hour. Uncover and bake 30 minutes longer or until meat is tender. **Yield:** 6 servings.

HAM PASTIES
Delores Yung, Watrous, Saskatchewan
(PICTURED ON PAGE 18)

5 cups all-purpose flour
1 tablespoon brown sugar
1 teaspoon salt
1/2 teaspoon baking powder
1 pound lard *or* shortening
1/2 to 3/4 cup cold water
1 egg, beaten
2 teaspoons vinegar
FILLING:
3 cups diced fully cooked ham (1/4-inch pieces)
2 tablespoons diced green pepper
2 tablespoons diced pimientos
1 tablespoon minced onion
1 can (10-3/4 ounces) condensed cream of mushroom soup, undiluted
GLAZE:
1 egg
1 tablespoon water
Poppy seeds *or* sesame seeds

In a large bowl, combine flour, brown sugar, salt and baking powder. Cut in lard, half at a time, until particles are the size of small peas. Combine 1/2 cup water, egg and vinegar; add all at once to flour mixture and stir with a fork just until dough holds together. Add remain-

ing water only if necessary. Form into a ball; wrap tightly and refrigerate for several hours. Meanwhile, combine all filling ingredients. On a lightly floured surface, roll out one-fourth of the dough to 1/8-in. thickness. Using a 3-1/2- to 4-in. round cutter, cut dough into circles. Place on ungreased baking sheets. Spread a scant tablespoon of filling on half of each circle. Moisten edge slightly with water and fold over, sealing with the tines of a fork. Cut slits in top of pasties. Repeat with remaining dough and filling. In a small bowl, beat egg with water; brush tops of pasties. Sprinkle with poppy or sesame seeds. Bake at 400° for 15-20 minutes or until golden. Serve warm. **Yield:** 3-1/2 to 4-1/2 dozen.

TEXAS-STYLE LASAGNA
Effie Gish, Fort Worth, Texas

1-1/2 pounds ground beef
1 teaspoon seasoned salt
1 package (1-1/4 ounces) taco seasoning mix
1 can (14-1/2 ounces) diced tomatoes, undrained
1 can (15 ounces) tomato sauce
1 can (4 ounces) chopped green chilies
2 cups (16 ounces) small-curd cottage cheese
2 eggs, beaten
12 corn tortillas (6 inches), torn
3-1/2 to 4 cups shredded Monterey Jack cheese

In a large skillet, brown meat; drain. Add seasoned salt, taco seasoning mix, tomatoes, tomato sauce and chilies; mix well. Simmer, uncovered, for 15 to 20 minutes. Combine cottage cheese and eggs. In a greased 13-in. x 9-in. x 2-in. baking dish, layer half of the meat sauce, half of the tortillas, half of the cottage cheese mixture and half of the Monterey Jack cheese. Repeat layers. Bake, uncovered, at 350° for 30 minutes or until bubbly. Let stand 10 minutes before serving. **Yield:** 10-12 servings.

Quick & Easy

CREAMED HAM AND ASPARAGUS
Linda Hartline, Marietta, Ohio
(PICTURED ON PAGE 19)

1 pound fresh *or* frozen asparagus, cut into 1-inch pieces
1 tablespoon cornstarch
1-1/2 cups milk, *divided*
2 tablespoons butter *or* margarine
1 teaspoon salt

1/2 teaspoon pepper
1/2 teaspoon dried parsley flakes
1-1/2 pounds fully cooked ham, cubed
3 hard-cooked eggs, chopped
2 cups (8 ounces) shredded cheddar cheese
Toast points *or* biscuits

In a saucepan, cook asparagus in a small amount of water until tender; drain and set aside. In a medium saucepan, mix cornstarch and 2 tablespoons milk. Add butter, salt, pepper and remaining milk; cook and stir over medium heat until thickened and bubbly. Add parsley, ham, eggs, cheese and asparagus; cook and stir over low heat until ham is warmed and cheese is melted. Serve over toast points or biscuits. **Yield:** 4-6 servings.

BREAKFAST HAM RING
Betty Becker, Columbus, Wisconsin
(PICTURED ON PAGE 18)

10 eggs
1 pound ground fully cooked ham
1 pound bulk pork sausage
1-1/2 cups soft bread crumbs
1/2 cup milk
2 tablespoons dried parsley flakes
1 tablespoon prepared horseradish

In a large bowl, lightly beat 2 eggs. Add the ham, sausage, bread crumbs, milk, parsley and horseradish; mix well. Press into a greased 6-cup ring mold. Bake at 350° for 1-1/4 hours. Toward the end of the baking time, prepare scrambled eggs with remaining eggs, seasoning as desired. Remove ring from oven and drain juices; unmold onto a serving platter. Fill the center with scrambled eggs. Serve immediately. **Yield:** 8 servings.

CREAMY NUTMEG CHICKEN
Candi Ondracek, Sacramento, California

6 to 8 chicken pieces, skinned
2 tablespoons butter *or* margarine
1/4 cup chopped onion
1/4 cup minced fresh parsley
2 cans (10-3/4 ounces *each*) condensed cream of mushroom soup, undiluted
1/2 cup sour cream
1/2 cup milk
1 tablespoon ground nutmeg
1/4 teaspoon rubbed sage
1/4 teaspoon dried thyme
1/4 teaspoon dried rosemary
Additional nutmeg

In a large skillet, brown chicken in butter. Remove chicken and set aside. In the same skillet, saute onion and parsley until onion is tender. Add soup, sour cream, milk, nutmeg, sage, thyme and rosemary; mix well. Return chicken to the skillet and spoon sauce over pieces. Simmer, uncovered, for 25-30 minutes or until chicken is no longer pink, basting occasionally. Sprinkle with nutmeg. **Yield:** 4-6 servings.

POPPY SEED CHICKEN
Janet Zoss, Jackson, Michigan

Quick & Easy

1 cup (8 ounces) sour cream
1 can (10-3/4 ounces) condensed cream of chicken soup, undiluted
1 tablespoon poppy seeds
1 teaspoon dill weed
4 cups diced cooked chicken *or* turkey
3 cups cooked rice
1-1/2 cups butter-flavored cracker crumbs
1/2 cup butter *or* margarine

In a large bowl, combine sour cream, soup, poppy seeds and dill; mix well. Stir in the chicken and rice. Spread into a greased 11-in. x 7-in. x 2-in. baking dish. Combine crumbs and butter; sprinkle over casserole. Bake, uncovered, at 350° for 30 minutes. **Yield:** 6-8 servings.

FESTIVE HAM GLAZE
Becky Magee, Chandler, Arizona
(PICTURED ON PAGE 19)

1 bone-in fully cooked ham (5 to 8 pounds)
1-1/2 cups orange juice
1-1/4 cups packed brown sugar
1 tablespoon grated orange peel
1 teaspoon dry mustard
1/4 teaspoon ground cloves

Score surface of ham, making diamond shapes 1/2 in. deep. Place in a large baking dish. In a bowl, mix remaining ingredients; pour over ham. Cover and refrigerate overnight, turning ham occasionally. Reserving glaze, remove ham to a rack in a shallow roasting pan. Insert meat thermometer. Bake, uncovered, at 325° until thermometer reads 140°, about 2-4 hours, brushing occasionally with glaze. **Yield:** 10-16 servings.

ADDED COLOR. To make the gravy in chicken-and-noodle dishes prettier, add a few drops of yellow food coloring.

SAUERKRAUT HAM BALLS
Lillian Thomas, Toledo, Ohio
(PICTURED ON PAGE 18)

1 pound ground fully cooked ham
1 can (16 ounces) sauerkraut, drained and chopped
1/4 cup finely chopped onion
3/4 cup plus 2 tablespoons dry bread crumbs, *divided*
1 package (3 ounces) cream cheese, softened
2 tablespoons chopped fresh parsley
1 tablespoon prepared mustard
1/4 teaspoon garlic powder
1/8 teaspoon pepper
1/4 to 1/2 cup all-purpose flour
2 eggs
1/4 cup milk
Oil for deep-fat frying

In a large bowl, combine ham, sauerkraut, onion and 2 tablespoons of the bread crumbs. In another bowl, combine cream cheese, parsley, mustard, garlic powder and pepper; stir into sauerkraut mixture. Chill for at least 1 hour or overnight. Shape into 1-1/4-in. balls; coat with flour. In a small bowl, beat eggs and milk. Dip ham balls into the egg mixture, then roll in the remaining bread crumbs. Heat oil to 375° in a deep-fat fryer or electric skillet; fry ham balls until golden brown. Drain. **Yield:** 8-10 servings. **Editor's Note:** Recipe can be made into 3/4-in. balls and served as an appetizer.

Quick & Easy

HAM AND CHEESE CALZONES
Shelby Marino, Neptune Beach, Florida
(PICTURED ON PAGE 18)

2 tubes (10 ounces *each*) refrigerated pizza crust
1 cup ricotta cheese
4 to 6 ounces sliced pepperoni
2 cups diced fully cooked ham
2 cups (8 ounces) shredded mozzarella cheese
Shredded Parmesan cheese, optional
Dried basil, optional
Meatless spaghetti sauce, warmed

Unroll one pizza crust, stretching gently to make a 14-in. x 11-in. rectangle. Spread half of the ricotta on half of the dough lengthwise, to within 1 in. of the edges. Sprinkle with half of the pepperoni, ham and mozzarella. Fold unfilled side of dough over filled half and press edges together firmly to seal. Transfer to a greased baking sheet. Repeat with remaining crust and filling ingredients.

Bake at 400° for 20-25 minutes or until golden brown. Sprinkle with Parmesan and basil if desired. Slice into serving-size pieces. Serve with spaghetti sauce. **Yield:** 8 servings.

HAMBURGER CASSEROLE
Helen Carmichall, Santee, California

✓ This tasty dish uses less sugar, salt and fat. Recipe includes *Diabetic Exchanges*.

2 pounds uncooked extra lean ground beef *or* ground round
4 pounds potatoes, peeled and sliced 1/4 inch thick
1 large onion, sliced
1 teaspoon salt, optional
1/2 teaspoon pepper
1 beef bouillon cube
1 cup hot water
1 can (28 ounces) tomatoes with liquid, cut up
Chopped fresh parsley, optional

In a Dutch oven, layer half of the meat, potatoes and onion. Sprinkle with half of the salt and pepper. Repeat layers. Dissolve bouillon in water; pour over all. Top with tomatoes. Cover and cook over medium heat for 45-50 minutes or until potatoes are tender. Garnish with parsley if desired. **Yield:** 10 servings. **Diabetic Exchanges:** One serving (without added salt) equals 2 starch, 3 lean meat; also, 314 calories, 277 mg sodium, 74 mg cholesterol, 33 gm carbohydrate, 28 gm protein, 8 gm fat.

ORANGE CHICKEN
Betty Sexton, Blairsville, Georgia

1 egg
1/3 cup orange juice
1 to 1-1/2 cups herb-seasoned stuffing mix, crushed
1 tablespoon grated orange peel
1-1/2 teaspoons paprika
1 teaspoon salt
8 boneless skinless chicken breast halves
6 tablespoons butter *or* margarine, melted
Orange slices, optional

In a shallow bowl, beat egg; add orange juice. In another bowl, combine stuffing mix, orange peel, paprika and salt. Dip chicken into the egg mixture, then into crumbs, turning to coat well. Pour butter into a 13-in. x 9-in. x 2-in. baking dish. Place chicken in baking dish, turning once to butter both sides. Bake, uncovered, at 375° for 45 minutes or until the chicken is tender and juices run clear. Garnish with orange slices if desired. **Yield:** 4-8 servings.

PLAN A PICNIC in your own backyard and be sure to "invite" these summertime specialties. This pleasing menu contains the most important food groups of all...main dish, side dish and dessert!

PICNIC LUNCH. Clockwise from bottom: **Santa Fe Chicken Heroes** (recipe on page 23), **Fresh Fruit Cobbler** (recipe on page 72) and **Spaghetti Salad** (recipe on page 31).

SWEET-AND-SOUR MEATBALLS
Kimmy Hubbard, Lodi, Ohio

1-1/2 pounds lean ground beef
2 eggs, lightly beaten
3/4 cup seasoned bread crumbs
2 tablespoons minced onion
1-1/2 teaspoons brown sugar
1 teaspoon salt
1/4 teaspoon ground nutmeg
1/8 teaspoon pepper
SAUCE:
1/2 cup packed brown sugar
2 tablespoons cornstarch
1 can (20 ounces) pineapple chunks, undrained
1/3 cup sliced green onions
1/3 cup vinegar
1 tablespoon soy sauce
1 green pepper, cut into strips
Hot cooked rice, optional

In a large bowl, combine the first eight ingredients; mix well. Shape into 2 dozen 1-1/2-in. balls. Place in a greased 2-qt. casserole. For sauce, mix brown sugar and cornstarch in a saucepan. Add pineapple and juice, green onions, vinegar and soy sauce; cook and stir until thickened and bubbly. Cook and stir 2 minutes more. Pour over the meatballs. Cover and bake at 350° for 40 minutes. Stir in green pepper. Return to the oven, covered, for 10 minutes. Serve over rice if desired. **Yield:** 6-8 servings.

STUFFED CHICKEN BREASTS
Jamie Harris, Bodega, California

 This tasty dish uses less sugar, salt and fat. Recipe includes *Diabetic Exchanges*.

4 skinless boneless chicken breast halves
1/2 cup diced fresh mushrooms
1/2 cup diced green pepper
1/4 cup diced onion
3 garlic cloves, minced
1/4 cup low-sodium vegetable *or* chicken broth
1 cup cooked rice
2 cups crushed cornflakes
1/2 teaspoon garlic powder
1/8 teaspoon cayenne pepper
1 cup skim milk

Pound chicken breasts to 1/4-in. thickness and set aside. In a saucepan, combine mushrooms, green pepper, onion, garlic and broth; bring to a boil. Reduce heat and simmer 3 minutes. Remove from the heat; add rice. Mix well and set aside. Combine cornflakes, garlic powder and cayenne pepper; mix well. Set aside. Spoon a fourth of the rice mixture onto the center of each chicken breast. Fold chicken around rice mixture; seal with toothpicks. Dip chicken in milk. Coat all sides with cornflake mixture. Place chicken in a shallow baking dish that has been coated with nonstick cooking spray. Spray tops of chicken with cooking spray. Bake at 375° for 55-60 minutes or until juices run clear. **Yield:** 4 servings. **Diabetic Exchanges:** One serving equals 3 starch, 3 lean meat, 1 vegetable; also, 399 calories, 572 mg sodium, 74 mg cholesterol, 55 gm carbohydrate, 34 gm protein, 4 gm fat.

Quick & Easy

SANTA FE CHICKEN HEROES
Bonnie Link, Goose Creek, South Carolina
(PICTURED AT LEFT)

6 boneless skinless chicken breast halves
1 tablespoon vegetable oil
1/4 to 1/2 teaspoon pepper
1/4 to 1/2 teaspoon crushed red pepper flakes
1/4 to 1/2 teaspoon chili powder
6 slices Monterey Jack cheese
6 French *or* Italian rolls, split
2 tablespoons butter *or* margarine, melted
Lettuce leaves and tomato slices
Salsa *or* picante sauce, optional

Pound chicken breasts slightly to flatten evenly. Brush both sides with oil. Combine seasonings; sprinkle on both sides of chicken. Grill over medium-hot coals for 6-8 minutes; turn and grill 4-6 minutes more or until chicken is tender and no longer pink. Top with cheese; allow to melt, about 2 minutes. Brush rolls with butter; grill just until toasted. Place lettuce, tomato and chicken on rolls; top with salsa or picante sauce if desired. **Yield:** 6 servings.

Quick & Easy

HEARTY HAM KABOBS
Gloria Houghton, Winter Park, Florida

1 green pepper, cubed
1 medium onion, cut into wedges
2 cups cubed fully cooked ham (1-1/2-inch pieces)
12 cherry tomatoes
1 can (20 ounces) pineapple chunks, drained
1 cup bottled Italian salad dressing
1 teaspoon Worcestershire sauce
Hot cooked rice

Blanch the green pepper and onion if desired. Thread alternately with the ham, tomatoes and pineapple onto four to six metal skewers. Combine the salad dressing and Worcestershire sauce; baste over kabobs. Broil or grill, bast-ing occasionally, until all ingredients are heated through, about 6-8 minutes. Serve over rice. **Yield:** 4-6 servings.

SALISBURY STEAK DELUXE
Denise Barteet, Shreveport, Louisiana

1 can (10-3/4 ounces) condensed cream of mushroom soup, undiluted
1 tablespoon prepared mustard
2 teaspoons Worcestershire sauce
1 teaspoon prepared horseradish
1 egg
1/4 cup dry bread crumbs
1/4 cup finely chopped onion
1/2 teaspoon salt
Dash pepper
1-1/2 pounds ground beef
1 to 2 tablespoons cooking oil
1/2 cup water
2 tablespoons chopped fresh parsley

In a bowl, combine the soup, mustard, Worcestershire sauce and horseradish; blend well. Set aside. In another bowl, lightly beat the egg. Add bread crumbs, onion, salt, pepper and 1/4 cup of the soup mixture. Add beef and mix well. Shape into six patties. In a large skillet, brown the patties in oil; drain. Combine remaining soup mixture with water; pour over patties. Cover and cook over low heat for 10-15 minutes or until meat is done. Remove patties to a serving platter; spoon sauce over meat. Sprinkle with parsley. **Yield:** 6 servings.

CHICKEN 'N' CHILIES CASSEROLE
Lois Keel, Albuquerque, New Mexico

1 cup (8 ounces) sour cream
1 cup light cream
1 cup chopped onion
1 can (4 ounces) chopped green chilies
1 teaspoon salt
1/2 teaspoon pepper
1 package (2 pounds) frozen loose-pack hash brown potatoes
2-1/2 cups cubed cooked chicken
2-1/2 cups (10 ounces) shredded cheddar cheese, *divided*

In a large bowl, combine sour cream, light cream, onion, chilies, salt and pepper. Stir in potatoes, chicken and 2 cups of the cheese. Pour into a greased 13-in. x 9-in. x 2-in. baking dish. Bake, uncovered, at 350° for 1 hour and 15 minutes or until golden brown. Sprinkle with remaining cheese before serving. **Yield:** 6-8 servings. **Editor's Note:** Cooked turkey or ham can be substituted for the chicken.

POOR MAN'S STEAK

Dorothy Bowen, Thomasville, North Carolina
(PICTURED AT RIGHT)

    1 cup water
    1 cup cracker crumbs
    1 teaspoon salt
    3 pounds ground beef
All-purpose flour
    2 to 3 tablespoons cooking oil
    1 can (10-3/4 ounces)
      condensed cream of
      mushroom soup, undiluted

In a large bowl, combine water, cracker crumbs and salt; add beef and mix well. Press into a 15-in. x 10-in. x 1-in. baking pan lined with waxed paper. Cover and refrigerate overnight. Cut the meat into 12 squares. Coat each square lightly with flour; brown in oil in a skillet, a few pieces at a time. Drain. Remove waxed paper from the baking pan; spread the soup in bottom of pan. Place meat squares in a single layer over soup. Bake, uncovered, at 300° for 35-40 minutes. To serve, spoon some soup over each meat square. **Yield:** 12 servings.

Quick & Easy

CURRIED TURKEY

Evelyn Gunn, Andrews, Texas

    2 cups milk
    2 chicken bouillon cubes
    2 cups diced peeled apples
    1 cup chopped onion
  1/4 cup cooking oil
    2 tablespoons all-purpose flour
    2 teaspoons curry powder
  1/2 teaspoon salt
  1/4 teaspoon pepper
    1 tablespoon lemon juice
    4 cups diced cooked turkey
Hot cooked rice

In a small saucepan, heat the milk and bouillon until bouillon is dissolved; set aside. In a large saucepan, saute apples and onion in oil until tender. Add flour, curry powder, salt and pepper; cook and stir until thick and bubbly. Gradually add milk mixture and lemon juice; mix well. Add turkey and heat through. Serve over rice. **Yield:** 4-6 servings.

LAMB NOODLE STROGANOFF

Margery Bryan, Royal City, Washington

    2 pounds ground lamb
    2 garlic cloves, minced
    1 can (16 ounces) tomato sauce
    1 teaspoon salt
  1/4 teaspoon pepper

    1 package (12 ounces) medium
      noodles, cooked and drained
    1 package (8 ounces) cream
      cheese, softened
    2 cups (16 ounces) sour cream
    6 green onions, sliced
1-1/2 cups (6 ounces) shredded
      cheddar cheese
Paprika

In a skillet, cook lamb and garlic until lamb is browned; drain. Stir in tomato sauce, salt and pepper. Simmer, uncovered, for 10 minutes. Place noodles in a greased 13-in. x 9-in. x 2-in. baking dish. Top with meat mixture. In a small mixing bowl, beat cream cheese and sour cream until smooth; stir in onions. Spread over meat mixture. Bake uncovered, at 350° for 30 minutes or until heated through. Sprinkle with cheese and paprika; let stand 5 minutes. **Yield:** 8-10 servings. **Variation:** Ground beef can be substitiuted for the lamb.

BARBECUED BEEF SANDWICHES

Denise Marshall, Bagley, Wisconsin
(PICTURED ON PAGE 40)

    2 pounds beef stew meat
    2 cups water
    4 cups shredded cabbage
  1/2 cup bottled barbecue sauce
  1/2 cup ketchup
  1/3 cup Worcestershire sauce
    1 tablespoon prepared
      horseradish
    1 tablespoon prepared mustard
   10 hamburger or other sandwich
      buns, split

In a covered Dutch oven or saucepan, simmer beef in water for 1-1/2 hours or until tender. Drain cooking liquid, reserving 3/4 cup. Cool beef; shred and return to the Dutch oven. Add cabbage, barbecue sauce, ketchup, Worcestershire sauce, horseradish, mustard and the reserved cooking liquid. Cover and simmer for 1 hour. Serve warm in buns. **Yield:** 10 servings.

BARBECUED STICKY RIBS

Jackie Remsberg, La Canada, California

  3/4 teaspoon garlic powder
    1 teaspoon salt
  1/2 teaspoon pepper
3-1/2 to 4-1/2 pounds pork
      spareribs (2 racks)
SAUCE:
    1 can (10-3/4 ounces)
      condensed tomato soup,
      undiluted
    1 small onion, chopped
    1 cup water

  1/2 cup light corn syrup
  1/2 cup ketchup
  1/4 cup cider vinegar
    2 tablespoons Worcestershire
      sauce
    2 teaspoons chili powder
    1 teaspoon hot pepper sauce
  1/2 teaspoon ground cinnamon

Combine garlic powder, salt and pepper; rub onto both sides of ribs. Place in a single layer in a 15-in. x 10-in. x 1-in. baking pan. Bake at 325° for 30-35 minutes; drain off fat. Combine sauce ingredients; pour over ribs. Bake 50-60 minutes longer, basting occasionally. Cut into serving-size pieces. **Yield:** 6-8 servings.

HAM AND CHICKEN CASSEROLE

Connie Sanden, Mentor, Ohio

    1 cup chopped onion
    2 tablespoons butter or
      margarine
    2 cups cubed fully cooked ham
    2 cups diced cooked chicken
    1 medium green pepper,
      chopped
  1/2 cup chopped sweet red
      pepper
    1 cup whole pimiento-stuffed
      green olives
    1 can (10-3/4 ounces)
      condensed cream of
      mushroom soup, undiluted
    1 cup (8 ounces) sour cream
1-1/2 teaspoons salt
  1/4 teaspoon pepper
    8 ounces noodles, cooked and
      drained
    3 tablespoons shredded
      Parmesan cheese

In a skillet, saute onion in butter until tender. In a large bowl, combine ham, chicken, peppers, olives, soup, sour cream, salt, pepper and onion. Fold in noodles. Pour into a greased 2-1/2-qt. baking dish. Sprinkle with the Parmesan cheese. Bake, uncovered, at 325° for 45 minutes or until bubbly. **Yield:** 8 servings.

GOLDEN OPPORTUNITY. Make your thick ham slices special by dusting them with flour, dipping them in a beaten egg and coating both sides with bread crumbs. Then brown in butter over moderate heat until both sides are golden.

WELCOME IN spring with this satisfying selection of enjoyable entrees. From the hot and juicy steaks to the slightly sweet pie, your gang is sure to ask for seconds.

BLOOMING WITH FLAVOR. Clockwise from bottom: **Poor Man's Steak** (recipe on page 24), **Scalloped Cheese Potatoes** (recipe on page 39), **Peanutty Pie** (recipe on page 73) and **12-Hour Salad** (recipe on page 33).

WHEN Jack Frost starts nipping at your nose, come in from the cold and warm up with a bowlful of steaming hot soup. Loaded with lots of hearty ingredients, soup makes a perfect anytime meal.

SOUPER SUPPER. Clockwise from bottom: **Tortilla Soup**, **Sauerkraut Soup** and **Country Fish Chowder** (all recipes on page 27).

Soups & Salads

Whether you serve them as a light main meal or a tasty first course, refreshing salads and hearty soups add special flair to your table.

TORTILLA SOUP
Pat Cox, Bogata, Texas
(PICTURED AT LEFT)

- 1 medium tomato, quartered
- 1 can (14-1/2 ounces) whole peeled tomatoes with liquid
- 1 small onion, quartered
- 1 garlic clove
- 2 cans (10-1/2 ounces *each*) condensed chicken broth, undiluted
- 1 tablespoon minced fresh cilantro *or* parsley
- 1/2 teaspoon chili powder
- 1/2 teaspoon salt
- 1/4 teaspoon pepper
- 1/4 teaspoon ground coriander
- 1/4 teaspoon ground cumin
- 6 corn tortillas (6 inches)
- 1/4 cup cooking oil
- Sour cream
- Shredded cheddar *or* Monterey Jack cheese

Place tomatoes, onion and garlic in a blender or food processor; blend until smooth. Transfer to a large saucepan. Add the chicken broth and seasonings; bring to a boil. Reduce heat and simmer for 3 minutes. Cut tortillas into 1/4-in. strips; fry in hot oil until crisp and brown. Drain. Ladle soup into bowls; top with tortilla strips, sour cream and cheese. **Yield:** about 4 servings (5 cups).

SAUERKRAUT SOUP
Thelma Leschenko, Edmonton, Alberta
(PICTURED AT LEFT)

- 2 pounds spareribs, trimmed
- 3 quarts water
- 2 cups diced peeled potatoes
- 2 carrots, chopped
- 1 teaspoon salt
- 1/2 teaspoon pepper
- 4 cups sauerkraut, rinsed and drained
- 1 pound smoked sausage, cut into 1-inch slices
- 5 bacon strips, diced
- 1 large onion, diced

In a large kettle or Dutch oven, cook ribs in water until tender, about 1-1/2 hours. Skim off foam. Remove ribs from broth; strain the broth and refrigerate. Remove meat from bones and set aside. When chilled, skim fat from broth. Return to the heat. Add potatoes, carrots, salt and pepper; simmer until vegetables are tender. Add sauerkraut, sausage and rib meat; simmer until heated through. Meanwhile, cook bacon until crisp; remove to paper towels to drain. Discard all but 1 tablespoon of the drippings. Cook onion in drippings until tender. Add to soup; simmer 20-30 minutes longer. Ladle into bowls. Garnish with bacon. **Yield:** 10-12 servings (3 quarts).

CRANBERRY MOUSSE
Helen Clement, Hemet, California

- 1 package (6 ounces) strawberry-flavored gelatin
- 1 cup boiling water
- 1 can (20 ounces) crushed pineapple
- 1 can (16 ounces) whole-berry cranberry sauce
- 3 tablespoons lemon juice
- 1 teaspoon grated lemon peel
- 1/2 teaspoon ground nutmeg
- 2 cups (16 ounces) sour cream
- 1/2 cup chopped pecans

In a large bowl, dissolve gelatin in boiling water. Drain pineapple, setting the pineapple aside and adding juice to gelatin. Stir in cranberry sauce, lemon juice, peel and nutmeg. Chill until mixture thickens. Fold in sour cream, pineapple and pecans. Pour into a glass serving bowl or an oiled 9-cup mold. Chill until set, at least 2 hours. **Yield:** 16-20 servings.

VEGETABLE MEDLEY SALAD
Esther Mishler, Hollsopple, Pennsylvania

- 1 medium head cauliflower, broken into florets and blanched
- 1 medium onion, sliced into rings
- 1 can (16 ounces) green beans, drained
- 1 can (16 ounces) wax beans, drained
- 1 can (16 ounces) lima beans, drained
- 1 can (16 ounces) kidney beans, rinsed and drained
- 4 sweet pickles, sliced
- 3 carrots, sliced and blanched
- 1-1/2 cups vinegar
- 3/4 cup water
- 1/2 cup sweet pickle juice, optional
- 2 cups sugar
- 1 teaspoon salt
- 1/2 teaspoon ground turmeric
- 1/4 teaspoon dry mustard

In a large bowl, combine cauliflower, onion, all of the beans, pickles and carrots. In a medium saucepan, bring remaining ingredients to a boil. Boil for 2 minutes, stirring occasionally. Pour over vegetables; stir gently. Cover and chill overnight. Stir again; drain before serving. **Yield:** 12-18 servings.

COUNTRY FISH CHOWDER
Linda Lazaroff, Hebron, Connecticut
(PICTURED AT LEFT)

- 1 cup chopped onion
- 1/2 cup finely chopped salt pork
- 3 tablespoons butter *or* margarine
- 3 cans (12 ounces *each*) evaporated milk
- 1 can (15 to 16 ounces) whole kernel corn, undrained
- 1 can (6-1/2 ounces) chopped clams, undrained
- 3 medium potatoes, peeled and cubed
- 1 teaspoon salt
- 3/4 teaspoon pepper
- 1 pound fish fillets (haddock, cod *or* flounder), cooked and broken into pieces
- Cooked crumbled bacon, optional
- Snipped chives, optional
- Additional butter *or* margarine, optional

In a large saucepan, cook onion and salt pork in butter until onion is tender. Add milk, corn, clams, potatoes, salt and pepper. Cover and cook over medium heat, stirring occasionally, until potatoes are tender, about 20 minutes. Stir in fish and heat through. Ladle into bowls. If desired, top with bacon, chives and/or a pat of butter. **Yield:** 8-10 servings (2-1/2 quarts).

BEEF AND ONION STEW
Lesa Swartwood, Fulton, Missouri

1-1/2 pounds beef stew meat
All-purpose flour
  1/4 cup butter *or* margarine
    3 cups diced onion
    1 garlic clove, minced
1-1/2 cups beef broth
    2 tablespoons cider vinegar
    1 tablespoon tomato paste
    1 bay leaf
1-1/2 teaspoons salt
    1 teaspoon lemon pepper
  1/2 teaspoon dried thyme
Cooked rice *or* noodles

Dredge meat in flour; brown in butter in a Dutch oven. Add the onion and garlic; cook, stirring occasionally, for 10 minutes. Add broth, vinegar, tomato paste and seasonings. Cover and simmer for 1-1/2 to 2 hours or until meat is tender. Serve over rice or noodles. **Yield:** 4-6 servings.

TANGY GERMAN POTATO SALAD
Thelma Waggoner, Hopkinsville, Kentucky
(PICTURED AT RIGHT)

    7 medium potatoes (about
      1-3/4 pounds)
    8 bacon strips
    1 small onion, chopped
  1/2 cup diced celery
    3 tablespoons all-purpose flour
    3 tablespoons sugar
  3/4 cup water
  1/2 to 3/4 cup vinegar
  1/4 to 1/2 teaspoon salt
Pepper to taste

Peel potatoes; place in a saucepan and cover with water. Cook until tender but firm. Meanwhile, in a skillet, cook the bacon until crisp. Drain, reserving 3 tablespoons drippings. Crumble bacon; set aside. In the drippings, saute onion and celery until tender. Add flour, sugar, water, vinegar, salt and pepper; cook and stir until mixture boils and thickens. Drain potatoes; slice and place in a large bowl. Add the bacon and sauce; toss gently to coat. Serve warm or at room temperature. **Yield:** 6 servings.

CAULIFLOWER SALAD
Paula Pelis, Rocky Point, New York

✓ This tasty dish uses less sugar, salt and fat. Recipe includes *Diabetic Exchanges*.

    1 medium head cauliflower, cut
      into florets
1-1/2 cups diced carrots
    1 cup sliced celery
  3/4 cup sliced green onions with
      tops
  1/2 cup sliced radishes
    1 carton (8 ounces) plain yogurt
    2 tablespoons white *or* tarragon
      vinegar
    1 tablespoon sugar
    1 teaspoon caraway seed
    1 teaspoon celery seed
  1/2 teaspoon salt, optional
  1/4 teaspoon pepper

In a large bowl, toss cauliflower, carrots, celery, green onions and radishes. Combine all of the remaining ingredients; pour over vegetables and stir to coat. Cover and chill for several hours. **Yield:** 12 servings. **Diabetic Exchanges:** One 1/2-cup serving (prepared with fat-free yogurt and without added salt) equals 1 vegetable; also, 22 calories, 22 mg sodium, trace cholesterol, 4 gm carbohydrate, 1 gm protein, trace fat.

CREAMED CABBAGE SOUP
Laurie Harms, Grinnell, Iowa
(PICTURED ON PAGE 16)

    2 cans (14-1/2 ounces *each*)
      chicken broth
    2 celery ribs, chopped
    1 medium head cabbage,
      shredded (3 pounds)
    1 medium onion, chopped
    1 carrot, chopped
  1/4 cup butter *or* margarine
    3 tablespoons all-purpose flour
    1 teaspoon salt
  1/4 teaspoon pepper
    2 cups light cream
    1 cup milk
    2 cups cubed fully cooked ham
  1/2 teaspoon dried thyme
Chopped fresh parsley

In a large soup kettle or Dutch oven, combine broth, celery, cabbage, onion and carrot; bring to a boil. Reduce heat; cover and simmer for 15-20 minutes or until vegetables are tender. Meanwhile, melt butter in a medium saucepan. Add flour, salt and pepper; stir to form a smooth paste. Combine cream and milk; gradually add to flour mixture, stirring constantly. Cook and stir until thickened; continue cooking 1 minute longer. Gradually stir into vegetable mixture. Add ham and thyme and heat through. Garnish with parsley. **Yield:** 8-10 servings.

GOLDEN GLOW SALAD
Thelma Waggoner, Hopkinsville, Kentucky
(PICTURED AT RIGHT)

✓ This tasty dish uses less sugar, salt and fat. Recipe includes *Diabetic Exchanges*.

    1 package (3 ounces)
      orange-flavored gelatin
    1 cup boiling water
    1 can (8 ounces) crushed
      pineapple
    1 tablespoon lemon juice
Cold water
  1/4 teaspoon salt, optional
  3/4 cup finely shredded carrots

In a bowl, dissolve gelatin in boiling water. Drain pineapple, reserving juice. Add lemon juice and enough cold water to pineapple juice to make 1 cup; add salt if desired. Stir into gelatin. Chill until slightly set. Stir in pineapple and carrots. Pour into an oiled 4-cup mold; cover and chill until firm. Unmold. **Yield:** 6 servings. **Diabetic Exchanges:** One serving (prepared with sugar-free gelatin and without added salt) equals 1/2 fruit; also, 35 calories, 42 mg sodium, 0 cholesterol, 8 gm carbohydrate, trace protein, 0 fat.

Quick & Easy

HAM PASTA SALAD
Deanna Mitchell, Independence, Kansas
(PICTURED ON PAGE 19)

    1 box (7 ounces) shell macaroni,
      cooked and drained
    2 cups cubed fully cooked ham
    1 cup chopped green pepper
    1 cup chopped tomato
  1/4 cup chopped onion
DRESSING:
  1/2 cup mayonnaise *or* salad
      dressing
  1/4 cup grated Parmesan cheese
    2 tablespoons milk
  1/4 teaspoon salt
Additional Parmesan cheese

In a large bowl, toss macaroni with ham, green pepper, tomato and onion. In a small bowl, combine mayonnaise, Parmesan cheese, milk and salt. Pour over pasta mixture and stir to coat. Cover and chill. Sprinkle with additional Parmesan before serving. **Yield:** 4-6 servings.

MEATY CHANGE. Substitute meatballs for stew meat in beef vegetable soup. Combine 1 pound of ground beef, 1 egg, 1-1/2 cups bread crumbs, salt, pepper and nutmeg to taste. Mix well; shape into 1/2-in. balls. Add to soup base, along with your vegetables, and cook for 30 minutes.

YOU JUST can't keep this mouth-watering meal under wraps! It's full of fantastic flavors that make it wonderful for everyday dinners or special occasions.

BIRTHDAY MEAL. Clockwise from top left: **Dad's Peach Ice Cream**, (recipe on page 73), **Tangy German Potato Salad** (recipe on page 28), **Barbecued Pork Sandwiches** (recipe on page 10) and **Golden Glow Salad** (recipe on page 28).

CANTALOUPE WITH CHICKEN SALAD

Elsie Trude, Keizer, Oregon

2 cups cubed cooked chicken
1-1/2 to 2 cups fresh blueberries
1 cup sliced celery
1 cup seedless green grapes, halved
1/2 cup sliced almonds
3 cantaloupe, halved and seeded

DRESSING:
1/2 cup mayonnaise
1/4 cup sour cream
1 tablespoon fresh lemon juice
1-1/2 teaspoons grated lemon peel
1-1/2 teaspoons sugar *or* sugar substitute to equal 1-1/2 teaspoons
1/2 teaspoon ground ginger
1/4 teaspoon salt, optional

In a large bowl, combine chicken, blueberries, celery, grapes and almonds. In a small bowl, mix dressing ingredients. Pour over the chicken mixture and toss gently. Spoon into cantaloupe halves. **Yield:** 6 servings. **Nutritional Information:** One serving (prepared with sugar substitute, light mayonnaise and light sour cream and without added salt) equals 285 calories, 87 mg sodium, 36 mg cholesterol, 37 gm carbohydrate, 18 gm protein, 9 gm fat.

CHEDDAR HAM CHOWDER

Ann Heine, Mission Hill, South Dakota
(PICTURED ON PAGE 19)

2 cups water
2 cups cubed peeled potatoes
1/2 cup sliced carrots
1/2 cup sliced celery
1/4 cup chopped onion
1 teaspoon salt
1/4 teaspoon pepper
1/4 cup butter *or* margarine
1/4 cup all-purpose flour
2 cups milk
2 cups (8 ounces) shredded sharp cheddar cheese
1 can (16 ounces) whole kernel corn, drained
1-1/2 cups cubed fully cooked ham

In a large saucepan, bring the water, potatoes, carrots, celery, onion, salt and pepper to a boil. Reduce heat; cover and simmer for 8-10 minutes or until vegetables are just tender. Remove from the heat; *do not drain.* Meanwhile, in a medium saucepan, melt the butter. Blend in flour. Add the milk all at once; cook and stir until thickened and bubbly. Add cheese and stir until melted. Stir into the undrained vegetables; return large saucepan to the heat. Add corn and ham; heat through, stirring occasionally. **Yield:** 6-8 servings (2 quarts).

BANANA SPLIT SALAD

Darlene Smith, Rockford, Illinois

1 can (8 ounces) crushed pineapple
2 cups water
1 package (3 ounces) lemon-flavored gelatin
8 large marshmallows
2 bananas, sliced
2 teaspoons lemon juice
1/4 cup sugar
5 teaspoons all-purpose flour
Dash salt
1 egg, beaten
1 tablespoon butter *or* margarine
1 cup heavy cream, whipped
1/4 cup chopped pecans

Drain pineapple, reserving 1/2 cup of juice; set aside. In a saucepan, bring water to a boil; remove from the heat. Add gelatin and marshmallows; stir until dissolved. Chill until partially set. Toss bananas with lemon juice; fold bananas and pineapple into gelatin. Pour into an 8-in. square dish. Chill until firm. Combine the sugar, flour and salt in a saucepan. Stir in egg and reserved pineapple juice; cook and stir over low heat until thickened. Remove from the heat; stir in butter. Cool. Fold in whipped cream; spread over gelatin. Sprinkle with pecans. Chill overnight. **Yield:** 9 servings.

HOT ASPARAGUS PASTA SALAD

Roberta Hulsizer, Yakima, Washington

1 package (8 ounces) corkscrew pasta
1 garlic clove, crushed
1/4 inch slice fresh gingerroot, minced, optional
1 tablespoon cooking oil
1 pound fresh asparagus, cut into 1-1/2-inch pieces
1/2 pound shrimp, peeled and deveined
2 tablespoons water
1/4 pound fully cooked ham, julienned *or* cubed
1 can (8 ounces) sliced water chestnuts, drained *or* 1 cup sliced celery
1/3 cup sliced ripe olives

DRESSING:
6 tablespoons vegetable oil
2 tablespoons white wine vinegar
1 tablespoon soy sauce
1/4 teaspoon salt
1/8 teaspoon pepper
1/8 teaspoon dry mustard

Cook the pasta according to package directions. Meanwhile, in a large skillet, saute garlic and gingerroot if desired in oil over medium-high heat for 1-2 minutes. Add asparagus, shrimp and water; cook until asparagus is crisp-tender and shrimp are cooked, about 8 minutes. Stir in ham, water chestnuts or celery and olives. Remove from the heat. Drain pasta and place in a large salad bowl; add asparagus mixture. Cover with foil. Combine dressing ingredients; pour over salad and toss. Serve immediately. **Yield:** 4-6 servings.

SPINACH SLAW

GaleLynn Peterson, Long Beach, California
(PICTURED ON PAGE 16)

8 cups shredded iceberg lettuce
5 cups shredded spinach
4 cups shredded red cabbage
3 cups shredded green cabbage
1 cup mayonnaise *or* salad dressing
1/4 cup honey
3/4 to 1 teaspoon garlic powder
1/2 teaspoon salt
1/4 teaspoon pepper

In a large bowl, toss lettuce, spinach and cabbage; cover and refrigerate. In a small bowl, combine remaining ingredients; cover and refrigerate. Just before serving, pour dressing over the salad and toss to coat. **Yield:** 12-16 servings.

HOLIDAY FRUIT SOUP

Eunice Jacobson, Wildrose, North Dakota
(PICTURED ON PAGE 59)

1 pound mixed dried fruit
3/4 cup small pearl tapioca
6 cups water, *divided*
5 apples, peeled and cubed
1 cup sugar
Ground cinnamon

Place fruit, tapioca and 4 cups water in a large saucepan. Cover and let stand overnight. Add apples, sugar and remaining water; bring to a boil. Reduce heat; cover and simmer for 1 hour or until tapioca is transparent. Add additional water if necessary. Serve warm or cold with a dash of cinnamon. **Yield:** 8-10 servings.

FROZEN WALDORF SALAD
Mildred Hall, Topeka, Kansas

- 1 can (20 ounces) crushed pineapple
- 1 cup sugar
- 2 eggs, beaten
- Dash salt
- 1 cup chopped celery
- 2 medium red apples, chopped
- 1 cup chopped pecans
- 1 cup heavy cream, whipped
- Lettuce leaves, optional

Drain pineapple, reserving the juice. Set pineapple aside. In a saucepan, combine juice with sugar, eggs and salt. Cook, stirring constantly, over medium-low heat until slightly thickened. Remove from the heat; cool. Stir in pineapple, celery, apples and pecans. Fold in whipped cream. Pour into a 9-in. square pan. Cover and freeze until firm. Let stand at room temperature for about 15 minutes before cutting. Serve on lettuce-lined plates if desired. **Yield:** 12 servings.

EASY SAUERKRAUT SALAD
Diane Hays, Morris, Minnesota

- 1 can (27 ounces) sauerkraut, rinsed and drained
- 1 cup finely chopped celery
- 1 cup finely chopped onion
- 1 jar (2 ounces) chopped pimientos, drained
- 1 cup sugar

In a large bowl, combine the first four ingredients. Pour sugar over and mix well. Cover and refrigerate overnight. Serve chilled. **Yield:** 8-10 servings.

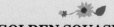

GOLDEN SQUASH SOUP
Nancy McFadyen, Smiths Falls, Ontario
(PICTURED ON FRONT COVER)

- 3 cups coarsely chopped onion
- 2 tablespoons cooking oil
- 1/4 teaspoon ground nutmeg
- 1/4 teaspoon ground cinnamon
- 1/4 teaspoon dried thyme
- 2 bay leaves
- 1-1/2 cups water
- 2 celery ribs, chopped
- 1 medium carrot, chopped
- 2 cups mashed cooked butternut squash, *divided*
- 1-1/2 cups tomato juice, *divided*
- 1 cup apple juice, *divided*
- 1 cup orange juice, *divided*
- Salt and pepper to taste

In a large saucepan or Dutch oven, saute onion in oil with nutmeg, cinnamon, thyme and bay leaves until onion is tender. Add water, celery and carrot; cover and simmer until carrot is tender. Discard bay leaves. In a blender container, place half of the squash and half of the tomato, apple and orange juices; add half of the vegetable mixture. Puree; return to pan. Repeat with the remaining squash, juices and vegetable mixture; return to pan. Add salt and pepper. Heat through. **Yield:** 6-8 servings (2 quarts).

Quick & Easy

SPAGHETTI SALAD
Kali Berry, Shawnee, Oklahoma
(PICTURED ON PAGE 22)

- 12 ounces thin spaghetti
- 1 bottle (8 ounces) Italian salad dressing
- 1 cup (4 ounces) shredded mozzarella cheese
- 1/2 cup diced pepperoni
- 1/2 cup diced fully cooked ham
- 1/2 cup chopped green pepper
- 1/2 cup diced tomato
- 1/2 cup chopped onion
- 1/2 cup chopped cucumber
- 1/4 cup sliced ripe olives
- 1 avocado, peeled and diced, optional

In a saucepan, cook spaghetti in boiling water until done. Rinse with cold water; drain well. Place in a large salad bowl and add remaining ingredients. Toss lightly to mix. Chill until serving. **Yield:** 15-20 servings.

HOLD THE SALT! Salt wilts and toughens salad greens, so be sure to only add salt to a green salad right before serving.

CHUNKY POTATO SOUP
Anne Kulick, Phillipsburg, New Jersey

- 1 medium onion, chopped
- 1 tablespoon butter *or* margarine
- 6 medium potatoes, peeled and cut into 3/4-inch cubes
- 2-1/2 quarts water
- 1/2 cup chopped celery leaves
- 1 tablespoon salt
- 1 teaspoon pepper
- 1 teaspoon paprika
- 1 can (8 ounces) tomato sauce
- 3 tablespoons vegetable oil
- 3 tablespoons all-purpose flour
- 2 to 3 tablespoons chopped fresh parsley

In a Dutch oven or large kettle, saute onion in butter for 3 minutes. Add potatoes, water, celery leaves, salt, pepper, paprika and tomato sauce; bring to a boil. Reduce heat; cover and simmer for 30 minutes or until potatoes are just tender, stirring occasionally. In a small skillet, combine oil and flour until smooth. Cook over medium heat, stirring constantly, until mixture is golden brown (watch closely to prevent burning). Carefully stir into hot soup. Add parsley. Cook, stirring occasionally, for 5 minutes or until soup thickens. **Yield:** 12 servings (3 quarts).

PUMPKIN VEGETABLE STEW
Gerald Knudsen, Quincy, Massachusetts

✓ This tasty dish uses less sugar, salt and fat. Recipe includes *Diabetic Exchanges*.

- 4 cups cubed peeled pumpkin *or* winter squash
- 1 can (14-1/2 ounces) tomatoes with liquid, cut up
- 1/2 cup chicken broth
- 2 cups fresh cut green beans (1-inch pieces)
- 1 cup fresh *or* frozen corn
- 1/2 cup sliced onion
- 1/2 cup chopped green pepper
- 1 garlic clove, minced
- 1/2 teaspoon chili powder
- 1/4 teaspoon pepper

In a large saucepan, combine all the ingredients. Bring to a boil. Reduce heat; cover and simmer for 40-45 minutes or until the vegetables are tender. **Yield:** 6 servings (2 quarts). **Diabetic Exchanges:** One serving (prepared with low-sodium broth) equals 1 starch, 1 vegetable; also, 83 calories, 109 mg sodium, trace cholesterol, 20 gm carbohydrate, 4 gm protein, 1 gm fat.

RUBY APPLE SALAD
Priscilla Weaver, Hagerstown, Maryland

- 1 package (3 ounces) cherry-flavored gelatin
- 2 tablespoons red-hot candies
- 1-3/4 cups boiling water
- 1-1/2 to 2 cups chopped apples
- 1/2 cup chopped celery
- 1/2 cup chopped walnuts

In a bowl, stir gelatin and candies in boiling water until dissolved. Chill until partially set. Fold in apples, celery and walnuts. Pour into a 1-qt. serving bowl. Chill until firm, at least 4 hours. **Yield:** 6-8 servings.

AFTER A DAY of frolicking in the snow, your clan will be hungry. Welcome them home with the aroma of simmering chili and freshly baked bread. Round out the meal with cool and colorful salad and homemade dessert.

WINTER WARM-UPS. Clockwise from top left: **Easy Cranberry Pie** (recipe on page 73), **Classic Chili** (recipe on page 33), **Cheddar Chive Bread** (recipe on page 46) and **Garden Olive Salad** (recipe on page 33).

12-HOUR SALAD
Dorothy Bowen, Thomasville, North Carolina
(PICTURED ON PAGE 25)

- 8 cups torn salad greens
- 1-1/2 cups chopped celery
- 2 medium green peppers, chopped
- 1 medium red onion, chopped
- 1 package (10 ounces) frozen peas, thawed
- 1 cup salad dressing *or* mayonnaise
- 1 cup (8 ounces) sour cream
- 3 tablespoons sugar
- 1 cup (4 ounces) shredded cheddar cheese
- 1/2 pound sliced bacon, cooked and crumbled

Place salad greens in the bottom of a 3-qt. bowl or 13-in. x 9-in. x 2-in. dish. Top with layers of celery, green peppers, onion and peas; do not toss. Combine salad dressing, sour cream and sugar; spread over salad. Sprinkle with cheese and bacon. Cover and refrigerate overnight. **Yield:** 12 servings.

Quick & Easy

SOUTHWESTERN RICE AND BEAN SALAD
Sherre Yurenko, Cypress, California

- 2 cups cold cooked long grain rice
- 1 can (16 ounces) kidney beans, rinsed and drained
- 1 can (8-3/4 ounces) whole kernel corn, drained
- 1/2 cup sliced green onions with tops
- 1/2 cup picante sauce
- 1/4 cup bottled Italian dressing
- 1 teaspoon ground cumin

Combine all of the ingredients in a large salad bowl. Cover and refrigerate until serving. **Yield:** 8-10 servings.

OLD-FASHIONED TOMATO SOUP
Wilma Miller, Port Angeles, Washington

- 1 can (14-1/2 ounces) tomatoes with liquid, cut up
- 1/2 teaspoon baking soda
- 1/4 to 1/2 teaspoon garlic salt
- 1/8 teaspoon pepper
- Salt to taste
- 1 quart milk
- 2 tablespoons butter *or* margarine
- Chopped fresh parsley, optional

In a large saucepan, bring tomatoes to a boil. Add baking soda, garlic salt, pep-

per and salt if desired. Reduce heat; add the milk and butter. Heat through but do not boil. Garnish with parsley if desired. **Yield:** 6 servings (1-1/2 quarts). **Editor's Note:** 2 cups of home-canned or freshly stewed tomatoes with liquid can be substituted for canned tomatoes.

GARDEN VEGETABLE SOUP
Dorothy Miller, Royersford, Pennsylvania

✓ This tasty dish uses less sugar, salt and fat. Recipe includes *Diabetic Exchanges.*

- 1 small head cabbage (about 1 pound), chopped
- 3 medium green peppers, chopped
- 2 medium sweet red peppers, chopped
- 5 medium onions, chopped
- 3 celery ribs, chopped
- 6 medium tomatoes, peeled, seeded and chopped *or* 1 can (28 ounces) tomatoes with liquid, cut up
- 4 cups chicken broth
- 1 bay leaf
- 1 tablespoon chopped fresh parsley *or* 1 teaspoon dried parsley flakes
- 1/4 teaspoon dried thyme
- 1/4 teaspoon garlic powder
- Salt and pepper to taste

Combine all ingredients in a large kettle or Dutch oven; bring to a boil. Reduce heat. Cover and simmer for 2-1/2 hours or until vegetables are tender, stirring occasionally. Remove the bay leaf before serving. **Yield:** 10 servings (about 3 quarts). **Diabetic Exchanges:** One serving (prepared with low-sodium chicken broth and without added salt) equals 1 vegetable, 1/2 starch; also, 64 calories, 39 mg sodium, 0 cholesterol, 15 gm carbohydrate, 4 gm protein, 1 gm fat. **If Cooking for Two:** Freeze soup in serving-size airtight containers to enjoy months later.

Quick & Easy

GARDEN OLIVE SALAD
Marjorie Carey, Belfry, Montana
(PICTURED AT LEFT)

- 1 medium head iceberg lettuce, torn
- 1 small onion, chopped
- 1 medium green pepper, chopped
- 2 cans (2-1/4 ounces *each*) sliced ripe olives, drained
- 4 medium tomatoes, cut into wedges
- 4 ounces Swiss cheese, cubed
- Salad dressing of your choice

In a large salad bowl, combine the first six ingredients. Add dressing and toss. Serve immediately. **Yield:** 6-8 servings.

CLASSIC CHILI
Marjorie Carey, Belfry, Montana
(PICTURED AT LEFT)

- 1 medium green pepper, chopped
- 2 medium onions, chopped
- 1/2 cup chopped celery
- 1 tablespoon cooking oil
- 2 pounds ground beef
- 2 cans (28 ounces *each*) tomatoes with liquid, cut up
- 1 can (8 ounces) tomato sauce
- 1 cup water
- 2 tablespoons Worcestershire sauce
- 1 to 2 tablespoons chili powder
- 1 teaspoon garlic powder
- 1 teaspoon dried oregano
- 1 teaspoon salt
- 1/2 teaspoon pepper
- 2 cans (16 ounces *each*) kidney beans, rinsed and drained

In a Dutch oven or large soup kettle, saute green pepper, onions and celery in oil until tender, about 5 minutes. Add ground beef and cook until browned; drain. Stir in tomatoes, tomato sauce, water, Worcestershire sauce and seasonings. Bring to a boil; reduce heat. Cover and simmer for 1-1/2 hours, stirring occasionally. Add kidney beans. Simmer, uncovered, 10 minutes longer. **Yield:** 10-12 servings (3 quarts). **If Cooking for Two:** Freeze in serving-size portions.

FOR GOODNESS SAKES SALAD
Olena Keef, Portland, Oregon

- 1 package (3 ounces) lemon-flavored gelatin
- 1 package (3 ounces) lime-flavored gelatin
- 1 cup boiling water
- 1 cup evaporated milk
- 1 can (20 ounces) crushed pineapple, undrained
- 1 cup mayonnaise
- 1 cup (8 ounces) cottage cheese
- 1 cup chopped nuts
- 1 tablespoon horseradish sauce

In a large bowl, dissolve the gelatins in boiling water. Cool slightly. Stir in the milk, pineapple with juice, mayonnaise, cottage cheese, nuts and horseradish sauce; mix well. Chill until partially set. Pour into an oiled 8-cup mold. Chill for 6 hours or overnight. Unmold. **Yield:** 12-16 servings.

CABBAGE FRUIT SALAD
Florence McNulty, Montebello, California
(PICTURED ON PAGE 40)

- 4 cups shredded cabbage
- 2 oranges, peeled and cut into bite-size pieces
- 2 red apples, chopped
- 1 cup seedless red grape halves
- 1/4 cup currants *or* raisins
- 1/2 cup mayonnaise *or* salad dressing
- 1/4 cup milk
- 1 tablespoon lemon juice
- 1 tablespoon sugar
- 1/8 teaspoon salt
- 1/2 cup chopped pecans, toasted

In a large bowl, toss cabbage, oranges, apples, grapes and currants; cover and refrigerate. In a small bowl, combine the mayonnaise, milk, lemon juice, sugar and salt; cover and refrigerate. Just before serving, stir dressing and pecans into salad. **Yield:** 6-8 servings.

Quick & Easy

FRESH FRUIT SALAD
Jane Zielinski, Rotterdam Junction, New York

- 4 cups fresh strawberries, halved
- 2 cups fresh blueberries
- 2 to 3 kiwifruit, peeled and sliced
- 2 bananas, sliced
- 2 cups seedless grapes, halved
- 1 carton (8 ounces) plain *or* vanilla yogurt
- 2 teaspoons lemon juice
- 1 teaspoon sugar
- 1/2 teaspoon vanilla extract

In a large salad bowl, combine strawberries, blueberries, kiwi, bananas and grapes. In a small bowl, combine yogurt, lemon juice, sugar and vanilla; mix well. Serve with fruit. **Yield:** 8-10 servings.

EGGPLANT SALAD
Elizabeth Roper, Norfolk, Virginia

✓ This tasty dish uses less sugar, salt and fat. Recipe includes *Diabetic Exchanges*.

- 1 medium eggplant (about 1-1/4 pounds)
- 4 medium tomatoes, cubed (3-1/2 to 4 cups)
- 3 hard-cooked eggs, cubed
- 1 large onion, chopped
- 1/2 cup prepared French salad dressing
- 1-1/2 teaspoons salt, optional
- 1/2 teaspoon pepper

Cut eggplant in half lengthwise. Place with cut side down in a greased 9-in.

square baking dish. Bake at 350° for 30-40 minutes or until tender. Cool, peel and cut the eggplant into 1/2-in. cubes; place in a large salad bowl. Add tomatoes, eggs and onion. Add dressing, salt and pepper; toss. Cover and chill 1 hour before serving. **Yield:** 10 servings. **Diabetic Exchanges:** One serving (made with low-fat dressing and without added salt) equals 2 vegetable and 1/2 fat; also, 76 calories, 268 mg sodium, 62 mg cholesterol, 10 gm carbohydrate, 3 gm protein, 3 gm fat.

Quick & Easy

GARDEN-FRESH SALAD
Donna Hess, Chambersburg, Pennsylvania
(PICTURED ON BACK COVER)

- 1 bunch leaf lettuce, torn
- 2 cups packed torn spinach
- 1 cup cubed mozzarella cheese
- 1/2 cup sliced celery
- 6 fresh mushrooms, sliced
- 5 bacon strips, cooked and crumbled
- 1 tomato, sliced

DRESSING:
- 1 cup vegetable oil
- 3/4 cup sugar
- 1/4 cup vinegar
- 1/4 cup minced onion
- 1 tablespoon Worcestershire sauce
- 1 tablespoon ketchup
- 1/4 teaspoon salt

In a large salad bowl, combine the first seven ingredients. Chill. Combine dressing ingredients; just before serving, pour over salad and toss. **Yield:** 6-8 servings.

BEAT THE HEAT. Add yogurt to soups seasoned with curry to reduce the "heat".

CRANBERRY/ORANGE MOLDED SALAD
Judy Kimball, Haverhill, Massachusetts

- 1 package (6 ounces) raspberry-flavored gelatin
- 2 cups boiling water
- 1 can (16 ounces) whole-berry cranberry sauce
- 1/4 teaspoon ground cinnamon
- Dash ground cloves
- 2 cups diced orange sections
- Lettuce leaves, optional

In a large bowl, dissolve gelatin in boiling water. Stir in cranberry sauce, cinnamon and cloves. Chill until partially set. Add the orange sections. Pour into an oiled 6-cup mold. Chill until set, about 3 hours. Unmold; serve on a lettuce-lined platter if desired. **Yield:** 8-10 servings.

HAM AND LENTIL SOUP
Andi Haug, Hendrum, Minnesota
(PICTURED ON PAGE 7)

- 1 meaty ham bone
- 6 cups water
- 1-1/4 cups dried lentils, rinsed and sorted
- 1 can (28 ounces) tomatoes with liquid, cut up
- 2 to 3 carrots, sliced
- 2 celery ribs, sliced
- 1/4 cup chopped green onions
- 1/2 teaspoon salt
- 1/2 teaspoon garlic powder
- 1/2 teaspoon dried oregano
- 1/8 teaspoon pepper
- 12 ounces bulk pork sausage, cooked and drained
- 2 tablespoons chopped fresh parsley

In a Dutch oven, bring ham bone and water to a boil. Reduce heat; cover and simmer for 1-1/2 hours. Remove ham bone. To broth, add lentils, tomatoes, carrots, celery, onions and seasonings; bring to a boil. Reduce heat; cover and simmer for 30-40 minutes or until lentils and vegetables are tender. Meanwhile, remove ham from bone; coarsely chop. Add ham, sausage and parsley to soup; heat through. **Yield:** 10-12 servings (3 quarts).

HAM AND CORN CHOWDER
Sharon Rose Brand, Stayton, Oregon

- 8 bacon strips, cut into 1-inch pieces
- 1 medium onion, diced
- 1 cup sliced celery
- 1/2 cup diced green pepper
- 3 cups cubed peeled potatoes (about 3 medium)
- 3 cups chicken broth
- 4 cups fresh *or* frozen whole kernel corn, *divided*
- 4 cups milk, *divided*
- 2 cups cubed fully cooked ham
- 2 tablespoons butter *or* margarine
- 3 tablespoons minced fresh parsley
- 1 teaspoon salt
- 1/8 teaspoon pepper
- 1/8 teaspoon hot pepper sauce, optional

In a large saucepan, cook bacon until crisp. Remove bacon to paper towel to drain, reserving 1/4 cup drippings in pan. Saute onion, celery and green pepper in drippings for 5 minutes. Add potatoes and broth. Reduce heat; cover and simmer for 10 minutes. Place 2 cups corn and 1/2 cup milk in a blender and process until pureed; pour into pan. Add ham and remaining corn; simmer for 10 minutes or until vegetables are tender. Stir in butter, parsley, salt, pepper, hot pepper sauce if desired and remaining milk; heat through. Garnish with bacon. **Yield:** 10-12 servings (3 quarts).

ZESTY POTATO SALAD
Dawna Nownes, Stratham, New Hampshire

8 medium red potatoes (about 2-1/2 pounds)
1 jar (6 ounces) marinated artichoke hearts, drained and quartered
1 can (4 ounces) chopped green chilies, drained
1 jar (4 ounces) diced pimientos, drained
1 medium green pepper, diced
1 medium sweet red pepper, diced
1 medium yellow pepper, diced
1/2 cup chopped red onion
1 teaspoon minced fresh basil *or* 1/2 teaspoon dried basil
Salt to taste
1 package (.6 ounce) zesty Italian salad dressing mix
1/3 cup vegetable oil
3 tablespoons white wine vinegar

Cook the potatoes until tender but firm. Drain and cube; place in a large bowl. Add artichokes, chilies, pimientos, peppers, onion, basil and salt. Combine remaining ingredients in a jar with a tight-fitting lid; shake well. Pour over salad and toss well. Chill at least 1 hour before serving. **Yield:** 10-12 servings.

CHERRY TOMATO SALAD
Sally Sibley, St. Augustine, Florida
(PICTURED ON PAGE 71)

1 quart cherry tomatoes, halved
1/4 cup vegetable oil
3 tablespoons vinegar
1/4 cup minced fresh parsley
1 to 2 teaspoons minced fresh basil
1 to 2 teaspoons minced fresh oregano
1/2 teaspoon salt
1/2 teaspoon sugar
Lettuce leaves

Place tomatoes in a shallow bowl. In a jar with a tight-fitting lid, combine the oil, vinegar, parsley, basil, oregano, salt and sugar; shake well. Pour over tomatoes. Cover and refrigerate overnight. Serve on a bed of lettuce. **Yield:** 6-8 servings.

Quick & Easy

BEEF AND CABBAGE STEW
Sharon Downs, St. Louis, Missouri
(PICTURED ABOVE)

1 pound ground beef
1/2 cup chopped onion
2 cans (16 ounces *each*) kidney beans, rinsed and drained
1 can (14-1/2 ounces) beef broth
1 can (16 ounces) crushed tomatoes
4 cups chopped cabbage
1/2 teaspoon dried basil
1/2 teaspoon dried marjoram
1/2 teaspoon dried thyme
1/2 teaspoon salt
1/8 teaspoon pepper

In a Dutch oven, cook beef and onion until meat is browned and onion is tender; drain. In a small bowl, mash 1/4 cup beans with 1/4 cup beef broth. Add to Dutch oven with remaining beans and broth, tomatoes, cabbage and seasonings. Cover and simmer for 30 minutes or until the cabbage is tender. **Yield:** 6-8 servings.

OLD-WORLD TOMATO SOUP
Linda Pandolfo, East Haddam, Connecticut

3 quarts water
4 beef short ribs (about 2 pounds)
2 to 3 meaty soup bones (about 2 pounds)
1 can (28 ounces) whole tomatoes with liquid
3 celery ribs, halved
1 large onion, quartered
1/2 cup chopped fresh parsley, *divided*

1 tablespoon salt
1-1/2 teaspoons pepper
4 carrots, cut into 1-inch pieces
2 parsnips, peeled and quartered
2 cups (16 ounces) sour cream
1/2 cup all-purpose flour
1/2 teaspoon ground nutmeg, optional
1 package (8 ounces) egg noodles, cooked and drained

In a large kettle, combine water, ribs, soup bones, tomatoes, celery, onion, 1/4 cup parsley, salt and pepper. Cover and simmer for 2 hours. Add carrots and parsnips; cover and simmer for 1 hour or until meat and vegetables are tender. With a slotted spoon, remove meat, bones and vegetables. Strain broth and skim off fat; return all but 1 cup broth to kettle. Set reserved broth aside. Remove meat from the bones; dice and return to kettle. Discard celery and onion. Cut parsnips, carrots and tomatoes into 1/2-in. pieces and return to kettle. Add remaining parsley. In a bowl, combine sour cream, flour, nutmeg if desired and reserved broth; stir into soup. Add noodles. Cook and stir until thickened and heated through (do not boil). **Yield:** 16-20 servings.

SWEETHEART SALAD
Arlene Hershey, Oxford, Pennsylvania

2 envelopes unflavored gelatin
1/4 cup cold water
1/2 cup sugar
1 can (20 ounces) crushed pineapple, undrained
2 tablespoons lemon juice
1/4 cup maraschino cherry juice
2 packages (3 ounces *each*) cream cheese, softened
12 maraschino cherries, quartered
2 to 3 drops red food coloring, optional
1 carton (12 ounces) frozen whipped topping, thawed
Lettuce leaves, optional

Soften gelatin in cold water. Meanwhile, in a saucepan, bring sugar and pineapple with juice to a boil, stirring until the sugar dissolves. Remove from the heat. Add gelatin and stir until dissolved. Add lemon and cherry juices. Cool to lukewarm. Whisk in cream cheese until thoroughly combined. Stir in the cherries and food coloring if desired. Chill until slightly thickened. Fold in whipped topping. Pour into an oiled 13-in. x 9-in. x 2-in. pan or 8-1/2-cup mold; chill until firm. Serve the mold or individual squares on lettuce-lined plates if desired. **Yield:** 12-16 servings.

REMEMBER Sunday dinners at Grandma's? Nothing could compare to fresh-from-the-oven bread and pleasing pot roast. And you'll never forget her homemade potato pancakes and skillet spinach dish.

SUNDAY BEST. Clockwise from bottom: **Savory Pot Roast** (recipe on page 10), **Cinnamon Raisin Bread** (recipe on page 47), **German-Style Spinach** (recipe on page 37) and **Onion Potato Pancakes** (recipe on page 37).

Side Dishes

Whether it's produce, potatoes or pasta, these scrumptious side dishes are sure to complement all of your family's favorite meals.

ONION POTATO PANCAKES
Joan Hutter, Warnick, Rhode Island
(PICTURED AT LEFT)

2 eggs
1 medium onion, quartered
2 tablespoons all-purpose flour
3/4 teaspoon salt
1/4 teaspoon pepper
1/4 teaspoon baking powder
4 medium potatoes, peeled and
  cubed (about 1-1/2 pounds)
2 tablespoons chopped
  fresh parsley
3 to 4 tablespoons
  cooking oil

In a blender or food processor, place the eggs, onion, flour, salt, pepper, baking powder and 1/2 cup of potatoes. Cover and process on high until smooth. Add parsley and remaining potatoes; cover and pulse 2-4 times until potatoes are chopped. Pour 1 to 2 tablespoons oil onto a hot griddle or skillet. Pour batter by 1/3 cupfuls onto griddle; flatten slightly to a 4-in. to 5-in. diameter. Cook over medium heat until golden on both sides. Add oil as needed until all pancakes are cooked. **Yield:** 6-8 servings (12 pancakes).

VEGETABLE NOODLE CASSEROLE
Tara Bricco, Covington, Tennessee

1 can (10-3/4 ounces)
  condensed cream of
  mushroom soup, undiluted
1 cup (8 ounces) sour cream
3/4 cup chopped onion
1 teaspoon salt
1/4 teaspoon pepper
1 package (10 ounces) frozen
  chopped broccoli, thawed
1 package (8 ounces) frozen
  cauliflower, thawed and cut
  into bite-size pieces
8 ounces wide egg noodles,
  cooked and drained
1-1/2 cups (6 ounces) shredded
  Swiss cheese, *divided*

In a large bowl, combine the soup, sour cream, onion, salt and pepper. Add the broccoli, cauliflower, noodles and 1/4 cup of cheese; mix gently. Pour into a

greased 13-in. x 9-in. x 2-in. baking dish. Top with remaining cheese. Bake, uncovered, at 350° for 30 minutes or until heated through. **Yield:** 6-8 servings.

 Quick & Easy

TEXAS POTATO WEDGES
Mildred Sherrer, Bay City, Texas

6 large potatoes
1 egg
1/3 cup milk
1-1/2 cups all-purpose flour
1-1/2 teaspoons paprika
1 teaspoon salt
1/2 teaspoon *each* dried thyme,
  basil, oregano and chili powder
1/4 teaspoon cayenne pepper
1/4 cup vegetable oil

Slice unpeeled potatoes into wedges (12-14 per potato). In a small bowl, beat egg and milk. In another bowl, combine flour and seasonings. Dip potato wedges into milk mixture; dust with flour mixture. Place in a single layer on an ungreased baking sheet. Drizzle with oil. Bake at 450° for 20-25 minutes or until golden brown and tender. **Yield:** 6-8 servings.

ITALIAN BAKED BEANS
Betty Stucky, Hutchinson, Kansas

6 ounces sliced pepperoni
1 medium green pepper,
  chopped
1 large onion, chopped
1 tablespoon butter *or*
  margarine
1 can (12 ounces) tomato paste
2 cans (4 ounces *each*)
  mushroom stems and pieces,
  undrained
1/2 teaspoon salt
1/2 teaspoon pepper
1/2 teaspoon garlic powder
1/2 teaspoon dried basil
1/2 teaspoon dried oregano
4 cans (16 ounces *each*) pork
  and beans
1/4 cup grated Parmesan cheese

In a Dutch oven, cook the pepperoni, green pepper and onion in butter until vegetables are tender. Stir in tomato paste, mushrooms, seasonings and beans; mix well. Sprinkle with Parme-

san cheese. Cover and bake at 350° for 50-60 minutes. **Yield:** 12-14 servings.

RED CABBAGE SIDE DISH
Elna Groot-Nibbelink, Bloomfield, Ontario

12 cups shredded red cabbage
2 apples, peeled and sliced
1/4 cup sugar
1/4 to 1/2 teaspoon ground
  cloves
1 bay leaf
3 tablespoons vinegar
1/4 cup water
1 tablespoon margarine
Pinch salt, optional

Place cabbage in a large saucepan; layer the apples over cabbage. Combine sugar and cloves; sprinkle over apples. Add bay leaf. Combine vinegar and water; pour over all. Place the margarine on top; add salt if desired. Cover and bring to a boil, stirring occasionally. Reduce heat; cover and simmer for about 1 hour. Uncover and simmer for 30 minutes or until liquid is absorbed, stirring occasionally. Remove bay leaf before serving. Serve warm. **Yield:** 12 servings. **Nutritional Information:** One serving equals 71 calories, 64 mg sodium, 0 cholesterol, 16 gm carbohydrate, 1 gm protein, 2 gm fat.

Quick & Easy

GERMAN-STYLE SPINACH
Joan Hutter, Warnick, Rhode Island
(PICTURED AT LEFT)

2 packages (10 ounces *each*)
  frozen chopped spinach
1 large onion, chopped
2 garlic cloves, minced
2 tablespoons butter *or*
  margarine
6 bacon strips, cooked and
  crumbled
1/2 teaspoon ground nutmeg
1/2 teaspoon salt
Pepper to taste

Cook spinach according to package directions. Drain well and set aside. In a large skillet, saute onion and garlic in butter until tender. Stir in the spinach, bacon, nutmeg, salt and pepper; heat through. **Yield:** 6-8 servings.

CABBAGE-POTATO SAUTE

Joann Jones, Ogema, Wisconsin

**4 cups shredded cabbage
1/2 cup water
1/4 cup grated raw potato
1 tablespoon margarine
Pinch salt and pepper
1 tablespoon vinegar**

In a saucepan, cook cabbage in water until tender, stirring occasionally; drain. Add potato, margarine, salt and pepper. Stir in vinegar. Cook and stir over low heat for 5 minutes. **Yield:** 4 servings. **Nutritional Information:** One serving equals 50 calories, 179 mg sodium, 0 cholesterol, 6 gm carbohydrate, 1 gm protein, 3 gm fat.

POTATO APPLE PANCAKES

Roberta Uhl, Summerville, Oregon
(PICTURED ON PAGE 49)

**2 large potatoes, peeled
2 medium apples, peeled
2 eggs, lightly beaten
1/4 cup finely chopped onion
2 tablespoons all-purpose flour
1 teaspoon salt
Cooking oil
Sour cream, optional**

Finely shred potatoes and apples; pat dry. Place in a bowl; add eggs, onion, flour and salt and mix well. In a skillet, heat 1/4 to 1/2 in. of oil over medium-high heat. Drop batter by heaping tablespoonfuls into hot oil. Flatten to form 3-in. pancakes. Fry until golden brown; turn and cook the other side. Drain on paper towels. Serve immediately with sour cream if desired. **Yield:** 10-12 pancakes.

GROUND BEEF DRESSING

Lynn Ireland, Lebanon, Wisconsin

 This tasty dish uses less sugar, salt and fat. Recipe includes *Diabetic Exchanges.*

**1 pound extra-lean ground beef
1 medium onion, chopped
1 medium apple, chopped
2 celery ribs, chopped
8 cups bread cubes
1 tablespoon poultry seasoning
1 teaspoon salt, optional
1/2 teaspoon pepper
2 cups low-sodium chicken broth**

In a skillet, brown beef; drain. Place in a large bowl; add remaining ingredients and mix well. Transfer to a 3-qt. baking dish that has been coated with nonstick cooking spray. Cover and bake at 325°

for 1-1/2 hours. Uncover and bake 10 minutes more or until dressing is lightly browned. **Yield:** 16 servings. **Diabetic Exchanges:** One serving (3/4 cup) equals 2 starch, 2 lean meat; also, 272 calories, 414 mg sodium, 18 mg cholesterol, 39 gm carbohydrate, 14 gm protein, 6 gm fat.

 Quick & Easy

CREAMY NOODLES AND CABBAGE

Gail Nero, Canton, Georgia

**6 tablespoons butter *or* margarine
1 small head cabbage, chopped (about 1 pound)
1 medium onion, chopped
1/4 teaspoon salt
1/4 teaspoon pepper
2 cups light cream
1 tablespoon all-purpose flour
1 package (12 ounces) noodles *or* fettuccine, cooked and drained
1 cup (4 ounces) shredded Parmesan cheese
1/2 cup crumbled cooked bacon**

In a Dutch oven, melt butter. Add cabbage, onion, salt and pepper. Cook and stir until vegetables are crisp-tender, about 10 minutes. Combine cream and flour. Add to vegetables; bring to a boil and boil 1 minute. Stir in noodles and Parmesan cheese; mix well. Pour into serving dish and sprinkle with bacon. Serve immediately. **Yield:** 10-12 servings.

FRUITED PEACH HALVES

Mrs. Damon Cross, Kenton, Tennessee

**1 can (29 ounces) cling peach halves (6 to 7 halves)
1/3 cup finely chopped dried apricots
1/4 cup finely chopped dried figs
1/2 cup finely chopped pecans, *divided*
Lettuce leaves**

Drain peaches, reserving 1 tablespoon juice in a bowl. Set peaches aside. To peach juice, add apricots, figs and 3 tablespoons pecans; mix well. Shape into 1-in. balls. Roll outside edges of peach halves in the remaining pecans. Place on a lettuce-lined salad plate; place a fruit ball on each. **Yield:** 6-7 servings.

SUNSHINE CASSEROLE

Gene Barnhart, St. Johns, Michigan

**2 cups finely shredded carrots
2 cups cooked rice
2 eggs, beaten
1-1/2 cups diced process American cheese
1 can (16-1/2 ounces) cream-style corn
1/4 cup milk
1 tablespoon butter *or* margarine, melted
1 tablespoon dried minced onion
1/2 teaspoon salt
1/4 teaspoon pepper**

Combine all ingredients in a 2-qt. baking dish. Bake, uncovered, at 350° for 35-45 minutes or until set. **Yield:** 6-8 servings.

OLD-FASHIONED CHEESE POTATOES

Martha Sue Stroud, Clarksville, Texas

**1/4 cup butter *or* margarine
1/4 cup all-purpose flour
2 teaspoons salt
1/2 teaspoon pepper
2-1/2 cups milk
1-1/2 cups (6 ounces) shredded process American cheese
6 medium potatoes, peeled and thinly sliced**

In a saucepan, melt butter. Add the flour, salt and pepper; cook and stir until a thick paste forms. Gradually add milk. Cook and stir until the mixture begins to thicken. Add cheese; cook and stir until melted. Place potatoes in a greased 13-in. x 9-in. x 2-in. baking dish. Pour sauce over potatoes. Bake, uncovered, at 350° for 1 hour or until potatoes are tender. **Yield:** 8-10 servings.

HOT PINEAPPLE SIDE DISH

Alice Blackley, Elkin, North Carolina

**1 can (20 ounces) pineapple chunks
1/2 cup sugar
3 tablespoons all-purpose flour
1/4 cup butter *or* margarine, melted
1-1/2 cups (6 ounces) shredded cheddar cheese, *divided*
2/3 cup coarsely crushed saltines (14 crackers)**

Drain the pineapple, reserving 1/4 cup of the juice; set aside. In a medium bowl, combine sugar and flour. Add the butter and 1 cup cheese; mix well. Gently stir in pineapple. Pour into a greased 1-1/2-qt. baking dish. Sprinkle crushed crackers on top; drizzle with reserved pineapple juice. Bake, uncovered, at 350° for 30-35 minutes or until bubbly around edges. Remove from the oven and sprinkle with the remaining cheese. **Yield:** 6 servings.

CRANBERRY APPLE RELISH
Bonnie Lee Morris, Chase, British Columbia

- 1 navel orange
- 4 cups fresh *or* frozen cranberries
- 4 large red apples, peeled and grated
- 2 cups sugar

Finely grate outer orange rind and set aside. Peel off and discard white membrane. Slice the orange into eight pieces. Place a fourth of cranberries and orange slices in a food processor or blender; process until evenly chopped. Transfer to a large bowl; repeat until all cranberries and oranges have been chopped. Stir in the rind, apples and sugar. Cover and refrigerate for at least 4 hours or overnight. **Yield:** 6 cups. **If Cooking for Two:** Relish will keep in an airtight container for 1 week in the refrigerator, or freeze in serving-size portions.

BAKED HOMINY AND CHEESE
Anna Allen, Owings Mills, Maryland

- 1 egg
- 2 cans (15-1/2 ounces *each*) white *or* yellow hominy, rinsed and drained
- 12 ounces process American cheese, cubed
- 3/4 cup milk
- 1/2 small onion, finely chopped
- 3 bacon strips, cooked and crumbled
- 1 tablespoon butter *or* margarine, melted
- 1/4 teaspoon pepper
Chopped fresh parsley, optional

In a large bowl, beat egg. Add hominy, cheese, milk, onion, bacon, butter and pepper; mix well. Spoon into a greased 11-in. x 7-in. x 2-in. baking dish. Bake, uncovered, at 350° for 45 minutes or until bubbly and top begins to brown. Let stand a few minutes before serving. Garnish with parsley if desired. **Yield:** 8 servings.

QUICK CORN. To microwave fresh corn, put two to four ears, with husks on, on a wet paper towel. Microwave on high for 4 minutes. Take out and let cool. Husk, holding ear with paper towel.

CROWN JEWEL PATTIES
Mary Jane Ruther, Trenton, New Jersey

- 1 egg
- 1/4 cup mayonnaise
- 1/2 cup finely chopped onion
- 2 tablespoons vegetable oil
- 1/4 teaspoon salt
- 1/8 teaspoon pepper
- 1-1/2 cups mashed cooked carrots
- 3 cups soft bread crumbs
- 2 cups crushed cornflakes

In a mixing bowl, beat egg. Add mayonnaise, onion, oil, salt, pepper and carrots; mix well. Add the bread crumbs and mix thoroughly. (If mixture is too wet to handle, add more crumbs.) Shape into 10 to 12 patties; coat with cornflakes. Place on a greased baking sheet. Bake at 375° for 25 minutes. **Yield:** 5-6 servings.

ASPARAGUS-STUFFED POTATOES
Helen Druse, Addieville, Illinois
(PICTURED ON PAGE 66)

- 4 medium baking potatoes
- 1 to 2 tablespoons milk
- 1/2 cup sour cream
- 1 teaspoon onion salt
- 1/8 teaspoon pepper
- 1 pound fresh asparagus, cut into 1-inch pieces and cooked
- 1 cup (4 ounces) shredded cheddar cheese
- 2 bacon strips, cooked and crumbled

Bake potatoes at 400° for about 1 hour or until done. Cut a thin slice off the top of each potato and discard. Carefully scoop out pulp while leaving shell intact. In a mixing bowl, mash pulp with milk, sour cream, onion salt and pepper until smooth. Fold in asparagus. Stuff shells; place in an ungreased shallow baking dish. Sprinkle with cheese and bacon. Return to the oven for 20-25 minutes or until heated through. **Yield:** 4 servings.

ONION PIE
Mary West, Marstons Mills, Massachusetts

- 6 to 8 medium onions, thinly sliced
- 2 tablespoons cooking oil
- 6 eggs
- 1 cup soft bread crumbs
- 1/2 cup grated Parmesan cheese
- 1/2 cup minced fresh parsley

In a large skillet, saute onions in oil until soft but not browned; drain well. In a mixing bowl, beat eggs. Add bread crumbs, Parmesan cheese, parsley and onions;

---

mix well. Place in a greased 10-in. pie pan. Bake at 350° for 35-40 minutes or until a knife inserted near the center comes out clean. **Yield:** 6-8 servings.

LIMA BEAN CASSEROLE
Margaret Taylor, West Haven, Connecticut

- 8 bacon strips, diced
- 1 medium onion, chopped
- 1 can (10-3/4 ounces) condensed tomato soup, undiluted
- 5 slices process American cheese, cut into 1/2-inch pieces
- 1 package (16 ounces) frozen baby lima beans, cooked and drained
Additional cheese slices, optional

In a large skillet, cook bacon until crisp. Remove to paper towel; drain, reserving 1 tablespoon of the drippings. Saute onion in drippings until tender. Stir in soup, cheese, beans and bacon. Cover and simmer over low heat for 5 minutes or until the cheese melts. Spoon into an ungreased 1-1/2-qt. casserole. Cover and bake at 350° for 20-30 minutes or until casserole is bubbly and beans are tender. Garnish with additional cheese if desired. **Yield:** 8-10 servings.

SCALLOPED CHEESE POTATOES
Dorothy Bowen, Thomasville, North Carolina
(PICTURED ON PAGE 25)

- 4 pounds potatoes, peeled and thinly sliced
- 2 cans (10-3/4 ounces *each*) condensed cream of mushroom soup, undiluted
- 1/4 cup butter *or* margarine, *divided*
- 2 cups (8 ounces) shredded sharp cheddar cheese, *divided*

In a large bowl, combine potatoes and soup. Layer half of the mixture in a greased 13-in. x 9-in. x 2-in. baking dish. Dot with half of the butter and sprinkle with half of the cheese. Repeat layers. Bake, uncovered, at 350° for 60-70 minutes or until the potatoes are tender. **Yield:** 12 servings.

ANY COUNTRY COOK will be delighted with the endless culinary possibilities that cabbage and sauerkraut offer. And your family will be "pungently surprised" with the wonderful flavor!

COLORFUL CREATIONS. Clockwise from lower left: **Reuben Baked Potatoes** (recipe on page 42), **Sauerkraut Stuffing** (recipe on page 10), **Barbecued Beef Sandwiches** (recipe on page 24), **Cabbage Fruit Salad** (recipe on page 34), **Cheddar Cabbage Wedges** (recipe on page 43), **Red Cabbage Casserole** (recipe on page 42), **Dilly Corned Beef and Cabbage** (recipe on page 8) and **Old-Fashioned Cabbage Rolls** (recipe on page 8).

CARROT CASSEROLE
Esther Mishler, Hollsopple, Pennsylvania

1 pound carrots, sliced
2 eggs
1/2 cup chopped onion
1 cup chopped celery
1 tablespoon chopped fresh parsley
3/4 cup butter *or* margarine, melted
1 teaspoon salt
8 cups cubed day-old bread

In a saucepan, cover carrots with water and cook until very tender. Drain and mash. In a large bowl, beat eggs; add onion, celery, parsley, butter and salt. Stir in carrots. Add bread cubes and mix well. Pour into a greased 2-qt. baking dish. Bake, uncovered, at 350° for 30-40 minutes or until set. **Yield:** 8-10 servings. **If Cooking for Two:** Freeze serving-size portions in airtight containers.

GLAZED BEETS
Rebecca Howard, Winona, Mississippi

1 can (16 ounces) sliced *or* diced beets
2 tablespoons sugar
1 tablespoon cornstarch
1/4 teaspoon salt
3 to 4 tablespoons vinegar
2 tablespoons butter *or* margarine

Drain beets, reserving 1/3 cup juice. In a saucepan, combine the sugar, cornstarch and salt. Stir in beet juice and vinegar; cook and stir over medium-high heat until thickened and bubbly. Cook and stir 2 minutes more. Add beets and butter; heat through. **Yield:** 4 servings.

REUBEN BAKED POTATOES
Erika Antolic, Vancouver, Washington
(PICTURED ON PAGE 40)

4 large baking potatoes
2 cups finely diced cooked corned beef
1 can (14 ounces) sauerkraut, rinsed, well drained and finely chopped
1/2 cup shredded Swiss cheese
3 tablespoons sliced green onions
1 garlic clove, minced
1 tablespoon prepared horseradish
1 teaspoon caraway seed

1 package (3 ounces) cream cheese, softened
3 tablespoons grated Parmesan cheese
Paprika

Bake the potatoes at 425° for 45 minutes or until tender. Cool. In a bowl, combine the corned beef, sauerkraut, Swiss cheese, onions, garlic, horseradish and caraway. Cut potatoes in half lengthwise. Carefully scoop out potatoes, leaving shells intact. Mash potatoes with cream cheese; stir into the corned beef mixture. Mound potato mixture into the shells. Sprinkle with Parmesan cheese and paprika. Return to the oven for 25 minutes or until heated through. **Yield:** 8 servings.

RED CABBAGE CASSEROLE
Julie Murray, Sunderland, Ontario
(PICTURED ON PAGE 41)

1 tablespoon shortening
8 cups shredded red cabbage
1 medium onion, chopped
1/2 cup lemon juice *or* vinegar
1/4 cup sugar
1 teaspoon salt
1 to 2 medium apples, chopped
1/4 cup red currant jelly
Lemon slices, optional

In a Dutch oven, melt shortening. Add the cabbage, onion, lemon juice or vinegar, sugar and salt; mix well. Cover and cook over medium heat for 10-15 minutes or until cabbage is crisp-tender, stirring occasionally. Add apples; cook 10-15 minutes more or until cabbage and apples are tender. Stir in jelly until melted. Garnish with lemon slices if desired. **Yield:** 8-10 servings.

POTLUCK POTATOES
Jane Carlovsky, Sebring, Florida

8 to 10 medium red potatoes (about 2 pounds)
1 jar (2 ounces) chopped pimientos, drained
1/2 cup chopped onion
1/8 teaspoon garlic salt
1/8 teaspoon onion salt
1 pound process American cheese, cut into 1/2-inch cubes
2 slices bread, cut into cubes
1/4 cup butter *or* margarine, melted

Place the unpeeled potatoes in a large saucepan and cover with water; cook until tender but firm. Drain; cut potatoes into 1-in. cubes. Place in an ungreased 2-1/2-qt. baking dish. Add pimientos, onion, garlic salt and onion salt; toss gently. Sprinkle with cheese. Place the

bread cubes on top and pour butter over all. Bake, uncovered, at 350° for 30 minutes or until bread is toasted. **Yield:** 10-12 servings.

CHEESE-STUFFED POTATOES
Pat Havey, Fort Pierce, Florida

2 large baking potatoes
1/2 cup sour cream
1/4 cup grated Parmesan cheese
4 bacon strips, cooked and crumbled
2 tablespoons finely chopped green onion
1 teaspoon prepared horseradish
Salt and pepper to taste
4 teaspoons butter *or* margarine
1/2 cup shredded sharp cheddar cheese

Bake potatoes at 425° for 45 minutes or until tender. Remove from oven; reduce temperature to 350°. Cut each potato in half horizontally; leaving a thin shell, carefully scoop pulp into a bowl. Set potato skins aside. To the pulp, add sour cream, Parmesan cheese, bacon, onion and horseradish. Mix with a fork until combined but not mashed. Add salt and pepper. Fill potato skins. Top each potato with 1 teaspoon butter and sprinkle with cheese. Place in a shallow baking dish. Bake at 350° until heated through, about 20 minutes. **Yield:** 4 servings.

SPICY RED CABBAGE
Lisa Gibbons, Wildwood, Illinois

2 jars (16 ounces *each*) sweet-and-sour red cabbage
5 bacon strips, cut into 1/2-inch pieces
1/2 cup chopped onion
2 small apples, peeled and diced
2 teaspoons vinegar
2 teaspoons brown sugar
Pinch ground cloves
3 tablespoons all-purpose flour

Drain cabbage, reserving liquid; set cabbage aside. Add enough water to liquid to equal 1-1/3 cups; set aside. In a large skillet, cook bacon until crisp. Remove bacon to paper towel to drain. Discard all but 1 tablespoon of the drippings. Cook the onion in drippings until tender. Add apples, vinegar, brown sugar and cloves. Combine flour with reserved liquid; pour into skillet. Bring to a boil; cook and stir 1 minute or until thickened. Stir in cabbage and bacon; heat through. **Yield:** 6-8 servings.

CRANBERRY NUT STUFFING
Judy Toth, Hyde Park, Ontario

2 medium onions, chopped
2 celery ribs, chopped
1/2 cup butter *or* margarine
6 cups cubed crustless day-old bread
1/2 cup chopped walnuts *or* hazelnuts
1-1/2 teaspoons poultry seasoning
1/2 teaspoon salt
1/2 teaspoon pepper
1 cup chopped fresh cranberries
3 eggs, beaten
1-1/2 cups chicken broth
2 tablespoons brown sugar

In a skillet, saute onions and celery in butter until tender; transfer to a large bowl. Stir in bread cubes, nuts, poultry seasoning, salt and pepper. Add cranberries; toss lightly to mix. In a small bowl, combine eggs, broth and brown sugar; pour over bread mixture. Mix lightly until bread is moistened. Place in a greased 2-qt. casserole. Cover and bake at 325° for 45 minutes. Uncover and bake 15 minutes more. Serve with turkey. **Yield:** 6-8 servings.

CHEDDAR CABBAGE WEDGES
Karren Fairbanks, Salt Lake City, Utah
(PICTURED ON PAGE 41)

1 medium head cabbage (3 pounds)
1/2 cup chopped green pepper
1/4 cup chopped onion
1/4 cup butter *or* margarine
1/4 cup all-purpose flour
1/2 teaspoon salt
1/8 teaspoon pepper
2 cups milk
3/4 cup shredded cheddar cheese
1/2 cup mayonnaise *or* salad dressing
3 tablespoons bottled chili sauce

Cut the cabbage into eight wedges, leaving a portion of the core on each wedge. Steam wedges in boiling salted water in a large kettle or Dutch oven for 10-15 minutes or until crisp-tender. Drain; remove core. Place the wedges in a greased 3-qt. baking dish. In a medium saucepan, saute the green pepper and onion in butter until tender. Stir in flour, salt and pepper and cook until bubbly. Gradually add milk; cook and stir until thickened. Pour over cabbage. Bake, uncovered, at 375° for 15 minutes. In a small bowl, combine cheese, mayon-

naise and chili sauce; spoon over wedges. Return to the oven for 5 minutes. **Yield:** 8 servings.

GREEN BEAN BUNDLES
Virginia Stadler, Nokesville, Virginia

1 pound fresh green beans, trimmed
8 bacon strips, partially cooked
1 tablespoon finely chopped onion
3 tablespoons butter, margarine *or* bacon drippings
1 tablespoon white wine vinegar
1 tablespoon sugar
1/4 teaspoon salt

Cook the beans until crisp-tender. Wrap about 15 beans in each bacon strip; secure with a toothpick. Place on a foil-covered baking sheet. Bake at 400° for 10-15 minutes or until bacon is done. In a skillet, saute onion in butter until tender. Add vinegar, sugar and salt; heat through. Remove bundles to a serving bowl or platter; pour sauce over and serve immediately. **Yield:** 8 servings.

BACON CHEESE POTATOES
Bertha Jensen, Mooresville, Indiana

8 to 10 medium potatoes (2-1/2 to 3 pounds)
1/2 cup finely chopped onion
1 pound process American cheese, cubed
1 cup mayonnaise
1/2 pound sliced bacon, cooked and crumbled
3/4 cup sliced ripe olives
Chopped fresh parsley, optional
Paprika, optional

Peel the potatoes; place in a saucepan and cover with water. Cook until tender but firm; drain and cube. In a bowl, mix potatoes with the onion, cheese and mayonnaise. Transfer to an ungreased 13-in. x 9-in. x 2-in. baking dish. Sprinkle with bacon and olives. Cover and bake at 350° for 30 minutes or until heated through. If desired, sprinkle with parsley and paprika. **Yield:** 8-10 servings.

CRAB-STUFFED POTATOES
Ruby Williams, Bogalusa, Louisiana

4 medium baking potatoes
1/4 cup butter *or* margarine
1/4 to 1/3 cup light cream
1 teaspoon salt
1/4 teaspoon pepper
1/4 cup finely chopped green onions *or* chives
1 cup (4 ounces) shredded cheddar cheese

1 can (6-1/2 ounces) crabmeat, drained, flaked and cartilage removed *or* 1 package (8 ounces) imitation crabmeat, cut up
Paprika

Bake potatoes at 425° for 45-55 minutes or until tender. When cool enough to handle, halve potatoes lengthwise. Carefully scoop out pulp into a bowl, leaving a thin shell. Set shells aside. Beat or mash potato pulp with butter, cream, salt and pepper until smooth. Using a fork, stir in onions or chives and cheese. Gently mix in crab. Stuff shells. Sprinkle with paprika. Return to the oven for 15 minutes or until heated through. **Yield:** 8 servings.

SCALLOPED CARROTS
Shelly Korell, Bayard, Nebraska

5 to 6 cups sliced *or* baby carrots
1 medium onion, diced
2 tablespoons butter *or* margarine
1 can (10-3/4 ounces) condensed cream of celery soup, undiluted
1 cup cubed process American cheese

Place carrots in a saucepan; cover with water. Cook until crisp-tender. Meanwhile, in another saucepan, saute onion in butter until tender. Add soup and cheese; stir until smooth. Drain carrots and add to cheese mixture. Transfer to a 1-qt. baking dish. Cover and bake at 350° for 15-20 minutes or until heated through. **Yield:** 6 servings.

WINTER SQUASH CASSEROLE
Glendora Hauger, Siren, Wisconsin

6 cups mashed winter squash
1/2 cup butter *or* margarine, melted
6 eggs, beaten
1 cup sugar
1/2 teaspoon salt
TOPPING:
1 cup packed brown sugar
1/2 cup butter *or* margarine, softened
1/4 cup all-purpose flour
1/2 cup slivered almonds

Combine first five ingredients; place in an ungreased 13-in. x 9-in. x 2-in. baking dish. Combine topping ingredients and crumble over the top. Bake, uncovered, at 350° for 45 minutes or until a knife inserted near the center comes out clean. **Yield:** 12 servings.

START SPREADING the hues! The different combinations and flavors of these colorful jams, jellies and preserves are going to delight you and your family all through the year.

BREAD SPREADS. Clockwise from lower left: **Christmas Jam**, **Cherry Almond Preserves**, **Blackberry Apple Jelly** and **Spiced Pear Jam** (all recipes on page 45).

Breads & Spreads

Nothing says "home" like the aroma of fresh-from-the-oven breads, muffins...and more! With such fantastic flavor, you'll want to keep plenty of these jams, jellies and preserves on hand.

CHERRY ALMOND PRESERVES
Connie Lawrence, Hamilton, Montana
(PICTURED AT LEFT)

    8 cups pitted sour cherries
      (about 4 pounds)
1-1/2 cups water
   10 cups sugar
    2 pouches (3 ounces *each*)
      liquid fruit pectin
    1 teaspoon almond extract

In a large kettle, bring the cherries and water to a boil; boil for 15 minutes. Add sugar and bring to a full rolling boil, stirring constantly. Boil for 4 minutes. Stir in pectin; return to a full rolling boil. Boil for 1 minute, stirring constantly. Remove from the heat; stir in extract. Skim off foam. Pour hot into hot jars, leaving 1/4-in. headspace. Adjust caps. Process 15 minutes in a boiling-water bath. **Yield:** 11 half-pints.

BLACKBERRY APPLE JELLY
Liz Endacott, Matsqui, British Columbia
(PICTURED AT LEFT)

    3 pounds blackberries (about
      2-1/2 quarts)
1-1/4 cups water
    7 to 8 medium apples
Additional water
Bottled apple juice, optional
  1/4 cup lemon juice
    8 cups sugar
    2 pouches (3 ounces *each*)
      liquid fruit pectin

In a large kettle, combine the blackberries and water; simmer for 5 minutes. Strain through a jelly bag, reserving juice and discarding pulp. Remove and discard stems and blossom ends from apples (do not pare or core); cut into small pieces. Place in the kettle; add just enough water to cover. Simmer until apples are soft, about 20 minutes. Strain through a jelly bag, reserving juice and discarding pulp. Measure the reserved blackberry and apple juices; return to the kettle. If necessary, add water or bottled apple juice to equal 4 cups. Stir in lemon juice and sugar.

Bring to a full rolling boil, stirring constantly. Add pectin, stirring until mixture boils. Boil for 1 minute. Remove from the heat; skim off foam. Pour hot into hot jars, leaving 1/4-in. headspace. Adjust caps. Process for 15 minutes in a boiling-water bath. **Yield:** about 9 half-pints.

CINNAMON RAISIN BISCUITS
June Mullins, Livonia, Missouri

    2 cups all-purpose flour
    1 tablespoon baking powder
    1 tablespoon sugar
    1 teaspoon ground cinnamon
  1/2 teaspoon salt
  1/2 cup shortening
  2/3 cup milk
  1/3 cup raisins
ICING:
    1 cup confectioners' sugar
1-1/2 tablespoons milk
  1/2 teaspoon vanilla extract

In a large bowl, combine flour, baking powder, sugar, cinnamon and salt. Cut in shortening until mixture resembles coarse crumbs. Add milk and raisins; stir only until combined. Turn dough onto a floured surface. Knead just until smooth, about 2 minutes. Roll to 1/2-in. thickness. Cut with a floured 2-1/2-in. round cutter; place on an ungreased baking sheet. Bake at 450° for 12-15 minutes or until golden. Meanwhile, combine the icing ingredients. Drizzle over warm biscuits. **Yield:** 8-10 biscuits.

SPICY APPLE BUTTER
E. Jane Layo, Waddington, New York

   18 medium tart apples (about 6
      pounds), quartered and cored
    3 cups apple juice
    3 cups sugar
    2 teaspoons ground cinnamon
  1/2 teaspoon ground cloves

In a large covered kettle, simmer apples in apple juice until tender, about 30 minutes. Press through a sieve or food mill. Return to kettle; boil gently for 30 minutes. Add sugar, cinnamon and cloves; cook and stir over low heat

for about 1 hour or until mixture reaches desired thickness, stirring more frequently as it thickens. Pour hot into hot jars, leaving 1/4-in. headspace. Adjust caps. Process for 10 minutes in a boiling-water bath. **Yield:** 8 half-pints.

CHRISTMAS JAM
Jo Talvacchia, Lanoka Harbor, New Jersey
(PICTURED AT LEFT)

    2 packages (20 ounces *each*)
      frozen whole strawberries
      or 2-1/2 quarts fresh
      strawberries
    1 pound fresh *or* frozen
      cranberries
    5 pounds sugar
    2 pouches (3 ounces *each*)
      liquid fruit pectin

Grind strawberries and cranberries in a food processor or grinder; place in a large kettle. Add sugar. Bring to a full rolling boil; boil for 1 minute. Stir in pectin; return to a full rolling boil. Boil for 1 minute, stirring constantly. Remove from heat. Cool for 5 minutes; skim off foam. Pour hot into hot jars, leaving 1/4-in. headspace. Adjust caps. Process for 15 minutes in a boiling-water bath. **Yield:** about 14 half-pints.

SPICED PEAR JAM
Karen Bockelman, Portland, Oregon
(PICTURED AT LEFT)

    8 cups chopped *or* coarsely
      ground peeled pears (about
      5-1/2 pounds)
    4 cups sugar
    1 teaspoon ground cinnamon
  1/4 teaspoon ground cloves

Combine all ingredients in a large kettle. Simmer, uncovered, for 1-1/2 to 2 hours or until thick, stirring occasionally. Stir more frequently as the mixture thickens. Remove from the heat; skim off foam. Pour hot into hot jars, leaving 1/4-in. headspace. Adjust caps. Process for 10 minutes in a boiling-water bath. **Yield:** 6 half-pints. **Editor's Note:** This recipe does not require pectin.

Quick & Easy

STRAWBERRY RHUBARB JAM
Deb Kooistra, Kitchener, Ontario
(PICTURED ABOVE)

2-1/2 cups fresh *or* frozen strawberries, crushed
1-1/2 cups finely diced fresh *or* frozen rhubarb
2-1/2 cups sugar
1 can (8 ounces) crushed pineapple, undrained
1 package (3 ounces) strawberry-flavored gelatin

In a large kettle, combine strawberries, rhubarb, sugar and pineapple. Bring to a boil; reduce heat and simmer for 20 minutes. Remove from the heat; stir in gelatin until dissolved. Pour into jars or freezer containers, leaving 1/2-in. headspace. Cool. Top with lids. Refrigerate or freeze. **Yield:** 5-1/2 cups.

CHEDDAR CHIVE BREAD
Marjorie Carey, Belfry, Montana
(PICTURED ON PAGE 32)

2 packages (1/4 ounce *each*) active dry yeast
2 cups warm water (110° to 115°)
5-3/4 to 6-1/4 cups all-purpose flour
3 cups (12 ounces) shredded cheddar cheese
1/2 cup chopped dried chives
1/4 cup butter *or* margarine, softened
1/4 cup sugar
1-1/2 teaspoons salt
1 teaspoon dried thyme

In a large mixing bowl, dissolve yeast in warm water. Add 3 cups flour, cheese,

chives, butter, sugar, salt and thyme; beat for 2 minutes. Stir in enough of the remaining flour to form a soft dough. Turn onto a floured board; knead until smooth and elastic, about 6-8 minutes. Place in a greased bowl, turning once to grease top. Cover and let rise in a warm place until doubled, about 1 hour. Punch dough down. Shape into two loaves and place in greased 9-in. x 5-in. x 3-in. loaf pans. Cover and let rise in a warm place until doubled, about 30 minutes. Bake at 350° for 40-45 minutes or until golden brown. Remove from pans to cool on a wire rack. **Yield:** 2 loaves. **If Cooking for Two:** Wrap one loaf in heavy-duty aluminum foil and freeze.

ONION HERB BREAD
Evette Nicksich, Bartlett, Nebraska
(PICTURED ON PAGE 9)

1 package (1/4 ounce) active dry yeast
1/2 cup warm water (110° to 115°)
1/2 cup warm milk (110° to 115°)
1 tablespoon butter *or* margarine
1 tablespoon sugar
1 teaspoon dried rosemary, crushed
1/2 teaspoon salt
1/2 teaspoon dill weed
1/2 teaspoon garlic powder
1/4 cup finely chopped onion
2-1/4 cups all-purpose flour, *divided*

In a mixing bowl, dissolve yeast in water. Add milk, butter, sugar, rosemary, salt, dill, garlic powder, onion and 1 cup of flour. Beat until smooth, about 1 minute. Add the remaining flour and stir for about 1 minute. Place in a greased bowl. Cover and let rise in a warm place until doubled, about 30 minutes. Stir down raised batter in about 25 strokes. Spread into a greased 8-1/2-in. x 4-1/2-in. x 2-1/2-in. loaf pan. Cover and let rise in a warm place until almost doubled, about 15 minutes. Bake at 375° for 40-45 minutes. Remove from pan; serve warm. **Yield:** 1 loaf.

GRANDMA'S CINNAMON ROLLS
Della Talbert, Howard, Colorado

DOUGH:
1 package (1/4 ounce) active dry yeast
1/4 cup sugar, *divided*
1 cup warm water (110° to 115°), *divided*

2 tablespoons butter *or* margarine, softened
1 egg
1 teaspoon salt
3-1/4 to 3-3/4 cups all-purpose flour
TOPPING:
1 cup heavy cream
1 cup packed brown sugar
FILLING:
1/2 cup sugar
2 teaspoons ground cinnamon
1/2 cup butter *or* margarine, softened

In a large bowl, dissolve yeast and 1/2 teaspoon sugar in 1/4 cup warm water. Add the remaining sugar and water, butter, egg, salt, and 1-1/2 cups of flour; beat until smooth. Stir in enough remaining flour to form a soft dough. Turn onto a lightly floured surface; knead until smooth and elastic, about 6-8 minutes. Place in a greased bowl, turning once to grease top. Cover and let rise in a warm place until doubled, about 1 hour. Meanwhile, combine topping ingredients; pour into a greased 13-in. x 9-in. x 2-in. baking pan; set aside. Combine filling ingredients; set aside. Punch dough down and turn onto a lightly floured surface. Roll into a 15-in. x 8-in. rectangle; spread filling over dough. Roll up from the long side. Seal seam. Slice into 15 rolls; place with cut side down over topping. Cover and let rise until nearly doubled, about 30-45 minutes. Bake at 375° for 25 minutes or until golden brown. Cool 3 minutes; invert pan onto a serving plate. **Yield:** 15 rolls.

SUGAR-FREE BLUEBERRY JAM
Fran Boise, Marian, New York

✓ This tasty dish uses less sugar, salt and fat. Recipe includes *Diabetic Exchanges*.

1/2 of a 6-ounce can frozen apple juice concentrate, thawed
1 envelope plain gelatin
5 cups fresh *or* frozen blueberries
1 tablespoon lemon juice
1/4 teaspoon ground nutmeg
1/8 teaspoon ground cinnamon

Pour the apple juice concentrate into a saucepan; sprinkle with gelatin and allow to soften for several minutes. Meanwhile, in a blender or food processor, finely chop blueberries, 1 cup at a time. Add lemon juice, spices and 2 cups of chopped berries to gelatin; heat over medium-low until gelatin is dissolved. Remove from the heat; stir in remaining berries and mix well. Pour into jars or plastic containers; store in the refrigerator up to 3 weeks. **Yield:** 4 cups. **Diabetic Exchanges:** One 1-tablespoon serving equals a free food; also, 12 calories, 1 mg sodium, 0 cholesterol, 3 gm carbohydrate, trace protein, trace fat.

SWEET POTATO BISCUITS
Vallie Williams, Smyrna, Georgia

2 cups self-rising flour*
1/8 teaspoon salt
1/2 cup shortening
1 cup mashed sweet potatoes
4 to 5 tablespoons milk

In a bowl, combine flour and salt. Cut in shortening and sweet potatoes until mixture resembles coarse crumbs. Stir in enough milk just until dough clings together. Knead lightly on a floured surface. Roll dough to 1/2-in. thickness. Cut with a 2-in. biscuit cutter and place on a lightly greased baking sheet. Bake at 450° for 12 minutes or until golden brown. (*If substituting all-purpose flour for self-rising flour, use 2 cups all-purpose flour, 1 tablespoon baking powder and an additional 1 teaspoon salt.) **Yield:** 1-1/2 dozen. **If Cooking for Two:** Freeze biscuits in freezer bags and thaw as needed.

CINNAMON RAISIN BREAD
Joan Hutter, Warnick, Rhode Island
(PICTURED ON PAGE 36)

 This tasty dish uses less sugar, salt and fat. Recipe includes *Diabetic Exchanges*.

2 packages (1/4 ounce *each*)
active dry yeast
1/3 cup warm water (110° to 115°)
5-1/2 to 6 cups all-purpose flour
1 cup warm milk (110° to 115°)
2 eggs, lightly beaten
1/2 cup sugar
6 tablespoons butter *or*
margarine, softened
1-1/4 teaspoons salt
FILLING:
1-1/3 cups light raisins
1-1/3 cups dark raisins
1 cup water
1/3 cup apple juice *or* cider
1 tablespoon ground cinnamon
1 egg, beaten

In a mixing bowl, dissolve yeast in water; let stand for 5 minutes. Add 2 cups flour, milk, eggs, sugar, butter and salt. Beat on medium speed for 2 minutes. Add enough remaining flour to form a soft dough. Turn onto a floured board; knead until smooth and elastic, about 6-8 minutes. Place in a greased bowl, turning once to grease top. Cover and let rise in a warm place until doubled, about 1 hour. Meanwhile, in a saucepan, bring first five filling ingredients to a boil. Reduce heat to medium; cook for 15-

20 minutes, stirring occasionally, or until almost all the liquid is absorbed. Remove from heat; set aside. Punch dough down and knead 1 minute. Place in same greased bowl; cover and let rise in a warm place until doubled, about 1 hour. Punch the dough down a second time and knead for 1 minute. Divide in half. Roll each half into a 12-in. x 8-in. rectangle; brush with egg. Spread half of filling over each rectangle to within 1/2 in. of edges. Roll up jelly roll fashion; pinch to seal. Place each loaf, seam side down, in a greased 9-in. x 5-in. x 3-in. loaf pan. Cover and let rise until doubled, about 1 hour. Bake at 350° for 35-40 minutes. Cover loosely with foil if top browns too quickly. Remove from pans to cool on a wire rack. **Yield:** 2 loaves (40 slices). **Diabetic Exchanges:** One serving (one slice) equals 1 starch, 1 fruit; also, 131 calories, 103 mg sodium, 11 mg cholesterol, 25 gm carbohydrate, 3 gm protein, 2 gm fat.

Quick & Easy

ZUCCHINI PINEAPPLE JAM
Kathy Weese, Jackson, Ohio

6 cups seeded, shredded,
peeled zucchini
6 cups sugar
1/2 cup lemon juice
1 can (20 ounces) crushed
pineapple, undrained
1 package (6 ounces)
strawberry-flavored gelatin

In a large kettle, bring the zucchini and sugar to a boil. Boil and stir constantly for 6 minutes. Add the lemon juice and pineapple; cook and stir for 8 minutes. Add gelatin; stir for 1 minute. Remove from the heat. Skim off any foam; fill jars or plastic containers. Cool before covering with lids. Refrigerate up to 3 weeks. **Yield:** 8-1/2 cups.

PEASANT BREAD
Sue Ann Chapman, Tulsa, Oklahoma

1 package (1/4 ounce) active
dry yeast
2 cups warm water (110° to
115°), *divided*
4 cups all-purpose flour
2 teaspoons salt
1 tablespoon sugar
1 tablespoon butter *or*
margarine, melted
1 tablespoon poppy seeds

Dissolve yeast in 1 cup warm water. In a large bowl, combine flour, salt and sugar. Add the yeast mixture and remaining water; stir until combined. Cover and let rise in a warm place until doubled, about 1 hour. Stir dough down. Divide in half.

Place each half in a greased 1-qt. round casserole or ovenproof bowl. Brush tops with butter and sprinkle with poppy seeds. Let rise in a warm place until doubled, about 45 minutes. Bake at 350° for 45 minutes. Remove from pans; serve warm if desired. **Yield:** 2 loaves.

APPLE RAISIN
COFFEE CAKE
Patricia Dzierwa, Dearborn, Michigan

1/2 cup shortening
1-1/2 cups sugar
1 egg
3 cups all-purpose flour
2 teaspoons baking powder
1/2 teaspoon salt
1 cup milk
1 cup raisins
2 baking apples, peeled and
sliced
2 tablespoons sugar
1 teaspoon ground cinnamon

In a large mixing bowl, cream shortening and sugar. Add egg and beat well. Combine the flour, baking powder and salt; add to creamed mixture alternately with milk, beating well after each addition. Stir in the raisins. Spread batter in a greased 13-in. x 9-in. x 2-in. baking pan. Top with apples. Combine sugar and cinnamon; sprinkle over the apples. Bake at 375° for 40-45 minutes or until cake tests done. Serve warm. **Yield:** 12 servings.

ZUCCHINI FRUIT
COCKTAIL LOAF
Margaret Sercer, Kansas City, Kansas

3 eggs
2 cups sugar
1 cup vegetable oil
2 teaspoons vanilla extract
2 cups chopped peeled zucchini
1 can (17 ounces) fruit cocktail,
drained
3 cups all-purpose flour
2 teaspoons baking soda
1-1/2 teaspoons ground cinnamon
1 teaspoon salt
3/4 teaspoon ground nutmeg
1 cup chopped walnuts

In a large mixing bowl, beat eggs. Add sugar, oil and vanilla; beat well. Stir in zucchini and fruit cocktail. Combine dry ingredients; stir into zucchini mixture. Stir in nuts. Pour into two greased and floured 8-in. x 4-in. x 2-in. loaf pans. Bake at 325° for 60-70 minutes or until bread tests done. Cool 10 minutes before removing from pans to a wire rack. **Yield:** 2 loaves. **If Cooking for Two:** Freeze one loaf to enjoy months later.

STRAWBERRY MARMALADE
Mrs. Craig Presbrey, Pascoag, Rhode Island
(PICTURED AT RIGHT)

2 medium oranges
2 medium lemons
1/2 cup water
1/8 teaspoon baking soda
1 quart ripe strawberries, crushed
7 cups sugar
1 pouch liquid fruit pectin (half of a 6-ounce package)

Peel outer layer of oranges and lemons; set aside. Remove the white membrane from fruit and discard. Set the fruit aside. Chop peels; place in a large saucepan. Add water and baking soda; cover and bring to a boil. Simmer for 10 minutes. Meanwhile, section oranges and lemons, reserving juice. Add fruit and juice to saucepan; cover and simmer for 20 minutes. Add strawberries. Measure fruit; return 4 cups to the saucepan. (If have more than 4 cups, discard any extra; if less, add water to equal 4 cups.) Add sugar and mix well. Boil, uncovered, for 5 minutes. Remove from the heat; stir in pectin. Stir for 5 minutes to cool; skim off foam. Pour into half-pint jars or freezer containers, leaving 1/4-in. headspace. Adjust caps. Process for 10 minutes in a boiling-water bath or store in the freezer. Serve with toast or biscuits. **Yield:** about 10 half-pints.

SUGAR-FREE PEAR BUTTER
Bonnie Haugen, Semmes, Alabama

 This tasty dish uses less sugar, salt and fat. Recipe includes *Diabetic Exchanges*.

4 quarts water
1/2 cup lemon juice, *divided*
4 pounds firm ripe pears (about 10 large)
2/3 cup white grape juice
2 teaspoons ground cinnamon
1 teaspoon ground cloves
1/4 teaspoon ground allspice
8 to 12 packets sugar substitute

In a kettle, combine water and 1/4 cup lemon juice. Peel, core and quarter the pears, placing them in lemon juice mixture to retard browning until all have been peeled. Drain liquid in kettle. Add grape juice and remaining lemon juice; bring to a boil. Reduce heat to medium; cook until pears are soft, about 20 minutes, stirring occasionally. Cool. Press through a sieve or food mill, or process in a blender or food processor until smooth. Return puree to kettle. Add spices; cook and stir until very thick,

20-35 minutes. Remove from heat; stir in sweetener. Adjust sweetener to taste. Pour into jars or plastic containers. Refrigerate up to 3 weeks. (For longer storage time, pour hot into hot jars, leaving 1/4-in. headspace. Process in a boiling-water bath for 10 minutes. Use within 3 weeks of opening.) **Yield:** 4 cups. **Diabetic Exchanges:** One 1-tablespoon serving equals 1/2 fruit; also, 26 calories, 1 mg sodium, 0 cholesterol, 7 gm carbohydrate, trace protein, trace fat.

MASHED POTATO MUFFINS
Judy Toth, Hyde Park, Ontario

1/2 cup all-bran cereal
3/4 cup sour milk
1 cup all-purpose flour
1/2 cup whole wheat flour
2 teaspoons baking powder
1 teaspoon baking soda
1 teaspoon salt
1/2 cup butter *or* margarine, softened
1/2 cup packed brown sugar
1 egg, beaten
1/2 cup leftover mashed potatoes
1/2 cup raisins

In a small bowl, combine bran and milk; let stand 10 minutes. Combine dry ingredients and set aside. In a mixing bowl, cream butter and brown sugar. Add egg, potatoes and bran mixture; beat until smooth. Stir in dry ingredients and raisins just until moistened. Spoon into 12 greased muffin cups. Bake at 375° for 20 minutes or until the muffins test done with a wooden pick. **Yield:** 1 dozen.

MORNING CRISPIES
Emily Goad, Franklin, Indiana
(PICTURED AT RIGHT)

1 package (1/4 ounce) active dry yeast
1/2 cup warm water (110° to 115°)
1 cup warm milk (110° to 115°)
2 cups sugar, *divided*
1/2 cup vegetable oil
1-1/4 teaspoons salt
2 eggs
1-1/2 teaspoons lemon extract
5-1/2 to 6 cups all-purpose flour
6 tablespoons butter *or* margarine, softened, *divided*
1 tablespoon ground cinnamon

In a large mixing bowl, dissolve yeast in water; let stand for 5 minutes. Add milk, 1/2 cup sugar, oil, salt, eggs, extract and 2 cups flour; beat well. Add enough remaining flour to make a soft dough. Turn onto a floured board; knead until smooth

and elastic, about 6-8 minutes. Place in a greased bowl, turning once to grease top. Cover and let rise in a warm place until doubled, about 1 hour. Punch the dough down. On a floured surface, roll out to a large rectangle 1/4 in. thick. Spread with 2 tablespoons butter and sprinkle with 1/3 cup of the remaining sugar. Fold dough in half lengthwise; roll out to 1/4-in. thickness. Spread with 2 tablespoons butter and sprinkle with 1/3 cup sugar. Fold in half widthwise; roll to 1/4-in. thickness. Spread with remaining butter and sprinkle with 1/3 cup sugar. Fold in half lengthwise; roll out to an 18-in. x 10-in. rectangle. Combine the cinnamon and remaining sugar; sprinkle half over the dough to within 1/4 in. of all edges. Starting with the shorter side, roll up tightly and pinch to seal. Cut into 1/2-in. slices and place on greased baking sheets (four to six slices per sheet). Cover with waxed paper and flatten with palm of hand. Sprinkle with remaining cinnamon-sugar. Let stand for 30 minutes. Bake at 400° for 12-15 minutes. Remove from baking sheets immediately. **Yield:** about 1-1/2 dozen.

GARLIC BUBBLE LOAF
Lynn Nichols, Bartlett, Nebraska

1 package (1/4 ounce) active dry yeast
1/4 cup warm water (110° to 115°)
2 cups milk
2 tablespoons sugar
1 tablespoon shortening
2 teaspoons salt
6-1/4 to 6-1/2 cups all-purpose flour
1/2 cup butter *or* margarine, melted
1 tablespoon dried parsley flakes
2 teaspoons garlic powder

In a mixing bowl, dissolve yeast in warm water. Let stand for 5 minutes. Add milk, sugar, shortening, salt and 2 cups flour; beat until smooth. Stir in enough of the remaining flour to form a soft dough. Turn out on a floured surface; knead until smooth and elastic, about 6-8 minutes. Place in a greased bowl, turning once to grease top. Cover and let rise in a warm place until doubled, about 1 hour. Combine melted butter, parsley and garlic powder. Punch dough down; divide into fourths. Divide each portion into 12 pieces. Roll each piece into a ball. Dip into the butter mixture and place in two greased 9-in. x 5-in. x 3-in. loaf pans. Pour any remaining butter mixture over dough. Cover and let rise until doubled, about 30 minutes. Bake at 375° for 35-40 minutes or until golden brown. Cool for 10 minutes. Remove from pans; serve warm. **Yield:** 2 loaves.

YOU DON'T need a special occasion to serve these breakfast or brunch favorites. Treat your family and friends to this delicious assortment today.

MORNING GLORY. Clockwise from bottom: **Ham a la King** (recipe on page 17), **Strawberry Marmalade** (recipe on page 48), **Potato Apple Pancakes** (recipe on page 38) and **Morning Crispies** (recipe on page 48).

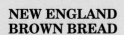

NEW ENGLAND BROWN BREAD

Rosemary Bouley, Worcester, Massachusetts
(PICTURED ON PAGE 59)

1/2 cup all-purpose flour
2 teaspoons baking soda
1 teaspoon salt
2 cups whole wheat flour
2 cups buttermilk *or* sour milk*
1/2 cup dark molasses
1 cup raisins

In a large bowl, combine all-purpose flour, baking soda and salt. In another bowl, combine whole wheat flour, buttermilk and molasses; add to flour mixture and mix well. Stir in raisins. Pour into two well-greased 5-1/4-in. x 3-3/4-in. coffee cans. Bake at 350° for 45-50 minutes or until breads test done. **Yield:** 2 loaves. (*To sour milk, place 2 tablespoons white vinegar in a measuring cup. Add enough milk to equal 2 cups.)

Quick & Easy

EASY APRICOT JAM

Geri Davis, Prescott, Arizona

16 ounces dried apricots
2-1/2 cups orange juice
3/4 cup sugar
1 tablespoon lemon juice
1/2 teaspoon ground cinnamon
1/4 teaspoon ground ginger

In a large kettle, combine apricots, orange juice and sugar. Cover and simmer for 30 minutes. Mix in lemon juice, cinnamon and ginger. Remove from the heat and cool to room temperature. Puree in a food processor or blender until smooth. Spoon into jars or freezer containers, leaving 1/2-in. headspace. Top with lids. Refrigerate or freeze. **Yield:** 4 cups.

OVERNIGHT SWEDISH RYE BREAD

Caroline Carr, Lyons, Nebraska

2 packages (1/4 ounce *each*)
active dry yeast
1/2 cup warm water (110° to 115°)
1 teaspoon sugar
4 cups warm milk (110° to 115°)
1 cup molasses
1 cup packed brown sugar
1 cup vegetable oil
1 cup quick-cooking oats
2 tablespoons grated orange
peel
1 tablespoon salt
1 teaspoon fennel seed

1 teaspoon aniseed
1 teaspoon caraway seed
2 cups rye flour
11 to 12 cups all-purpose flour

In a large mixing bowl, dissolve yeast in water; stir in sugar and let stand for 5 minutes. Add milk, molasses, brown sugar, oil, oats, orange peel, salt, fennel, aniseed, caraway, rye flour and 6 cups of all-purpose flour. Add enough remaining all-purpose flour to form a soft but sticky dough. Cover and let rise in a warm place overnight. Punch dough down. Turn onto a floured board; knead until smooth and elastic, about 6-8 minutes. Shape into four loaves. Place in greased 9-in. x 5-in. x 3-in. loaf pans. Cover and let rise until doubled, about 1 hour. Bake at 350° for 35-45 minutes. Remove from the pans to cool on wire racks. **Yield:** 4 loaves.

CHEESE SNACK BREAD

Fern Mumford, Chicago Heights, Illinois

1 package (1/4 ounce) active
dry yeast
1/4 cup warm water (110° to 115°)
3/4 cup warm milk (110° to 115°)
2 tablespoons shortening
1 tablespoon sugar
1 tablespoon salt
2-1/4 to 2-3/4 cups all-purpose flour
TOPPING:
2 cups (8 ounces) shredded
process American cheese
1 egg, beaten
1/3 cup milk
1 teaspoon minced onion
Caraway seeds *or* poppy seeds

In a large mixing bowl, dissolve yeast in warm water; let stand for 5 minutes. Add warm milk, shortening, sugar, salt and 1-1/4 cups flour. Beat until smooth; stir in enough remaining flour to form a soft dough. Turn onto a lightly floured surface; knead until smooth and elastic, about 5 minutes. Place in a greased bowl, turning once to grease top. Cover and let rise in a warm place until doubled, about 1 hour. Punch dough down. Pat into a greased 15-in. x 10-in. x 1-in. baking pan. Cover and let rise in a warm place until doubled, about 30 minutes. Meanwhile, combine cheese, egg, milk and onion. Spread over dough. Sprinkle with caraway seeds or poppy seeds. Bake at 375° for 20 minutes or until golden brown. Cut into squares and serve warm. **Yield:** 20-25 servings.

PRESERVE YOUR TIME. In summer, freeze most of your fruit and juices—then turn them into jams and jellies in the fall and winter when you're not as busy.

PUMPKIN GINGERBREAD

Mrs. Edwin Hill, Santa Barbara, California

1 cup all-purpose flour, *divided*
1/4 cup packed brown sugar
1 teaspoon baking powder
1/4 teaspoon baking soda
1/2 teaspoon ground cinnamon
1/2 teaspoon ground ginger
1/4 cup canned pumpkin
1/4 cup molasses
1 egg
2-1/2 tablespoons butter *or*
margarine
2 tablespoons milk
TOPPING:
1/3 cup chopped walnuts
1 tablespoon sugar

In a mixing bowl, combine 1/2 cup flour, brown sugar, baking powder, baking soda, cinnamon and ginger. Add pumpkin, molasses, egg, butter and milk. Beat on low speed for 30 seconds, then on high for 2 minutes. Add the remaining flour; beat on high for 2 minutes. Pour into two greased 4-1/2-in. x 2-1/2-in. x 1-1/2-in. loaf pans. (There will be a small amount of dough in each pan.) Combine topping ingredients; sprinkle over batter. Bake at 350° for 35-40 minutes or until a toothpick inserted near the center comes out clean. Cool 10 minutes in pans before removing to wire racks. Cool completely. **Yield:** 2 mini loaves.

Quick & Easy

CIDER JELLY

Donna Bensend, Dallas, Wisconsin

1 quart apple cider
2/3 cup red-hot candies
1 package (1-3/4 ounces)
powdered fruit pectin
5 cups sugar

In a large kettle, heat cider, candies and pectin, stirring often. Bring to a full rolling boil. Add sugar; return to a full rolling boil, stirring constantly. Boil for 1 minute. Remove from the heat; skim off any foam. Pour hot into hot jars, leaving 1/4-in. headspace. Adjust caps. Process for 10 minutes in a boiling-water bath. **Yield:** about 6 half-pints.

ENGLISH MUFFIN BREAD

Jane Zielinski, Rotterdam Junction, New York

5 cups all-purpose flour, *divided*
2 packages (1/4 ounce *each*)
active dry yeast
1 tablespoon sugar
2 teaspoons salt
1/4 teaspoon baking soda

2 cups warm milk (120° to 130°)
1/2 cup warm water (120° to 130°)
Cornmeal

In a large mixing bowl, combine 2 cups flour, yeast, sugar, salt and baking soda. Add warm milk and water; beat on low speed for 30 seconds, scraping bowl occasionally. Beat on high for 3 minutes. Stir in remaining flour (batter will be stiff). *Do not knead.* Grease two 8-1/2-in. x 4-1/2-in. x 2-1/2-in. loaf pans. Sprinkle pans with cornmeal. Spoon batter into the pans and sprinkle cornmeal on top. Cover and let rise in a warm place until doubled, about 45 minutes. Bake at 375° for 35 minutes or until golden brown. Remove from pans immediately and cool on wire racks. Slice and toast. **Yield:** 2 loaves. **If Cooking for Two:** Freeze one loaf to enjoy weeks later.

PINEAPPLE CARROT BREAD
Paula Spink, Elkins Park, Pennsylvania

3 cups all-purpose flour
2 cups sugar
1 teaspoon baking soda
1 teaspoon ground cinnamon
3/4 teaspoon salt
3 eggs
2 cups shredded carrots
1 cup vegetable oil
1 can (8 ounces) crushed pineapple, drained
1 cup chopped pecans *or* walnuts
2 teaspoons vanilla extract
3/4 cup confectioners' sugar, optional
1 to 1-1/2 teaspoons milk, optional

In a large bowl, combine the flour, sugar, baking soda, cinnamon and salt. In another bowl, beat eggs; add carrots, oil, pineapple, nuts and vanilla. Stir into the dry ingredients just until moistened. Spoon into two greased and floured 8-1/2-in. x 4-1/2-in. x 2-1/2-in. loaf pans. Bake at 350° for 65-75 minutes or until loaves test done. Cool 10 minutes in pans before removing to wire racks. Cool completely. If desired, combine confectioners' sugar and milk; drizzle over loaves. **Yield:** 2 loaves.

Quick & Easy

ALMOST RASPBERRY JAM
Sue Ellen Dillard, El Dorado, Arkansas

5-1/2 cups chopped green tomatoes
5-1/2 cups sugar
1 package (6 ounces) raspberry-flavored gelatin

In a large kettle, combine tomatoes and sugar. Simmer for 25 minutes, stirring occasionally. Remove from the heat; stir in gelatin until dissolved, about 1 minute. Pour into jars or plastic containers; cool, stirring occasionally to prevent floating fruit. Top with lids. Refrigerate up to 3 weeks. **Yield:** 7 cups.

AUNT MARY'S BANANA-CHOCOLATE CHIP BREAD
Sandra Flick, Toledo, Ohio

1 cup sugar
1/2 cup shortening
2 eggs
2 teaspoons vanilla extract
2 bananas, mashed (about 3/4 cup)
2 cups all-purpose flour
1 teaspoon baking soda
1/2 teaspoon salt
1 cup (6 ounces) semisweet chocolate chips

In a mixing bowl, cream sugar and shortening. Beat in eggs, vanilla and bananas until thoroughly blended. Combine flour, baking soda and salt; add to creamed mixture and stir just until combined. Fold in chocolate chips. Spoon into a greased 9-in. x 5-in. x 3-in. loaf pan. Bake at 350° for 60-70 minutes or until the bread tests done with a wooden pick. Cool in pan for 10 minutes before removing to a wire rack to cool completely. **Yield:** 1 loaf. **If Cooking for Two:** Freeze slices in freezer bags or wrapped in foil.

SUNSHINE MUFFINS
Sharyn Browning, Loxahatchee, Florida
(PICTURED ON BACK COVER)

1-1/2 cups all-purpose flour
1 cup whole wheat flour
1-2/3 cups sugar
2 teaspoons baking powder
1/2 teaspoon salt
3/4 cup butter *or* margarine, melted
3 eggs, beaten
2/3 cup fresh orange juice
1 teaspoon vanilla extract
1 teaspoon orange extract
1 tablespoon orange marmalade
1/2 cup chopped walnuts

In a large bowl, combine flours, sugar, baking powder and salt. Add remaining ingredients; stir just until moistened (batter may be lumpy). Fill greased or paper-lined muffin cups two-thirds full. Bake at 350° for 15-20 minutes or until top of muffin springs back when lightly touched. **Yield:** 15-18 muffins.

OATMEAL MOLASSES BREAD
Nita Baird, Wibaux, Montana

2 cups boiling water
1 cup old-fashioned oats
2 packages (1/4 ounce *each*) active dry yeast
1/3 cup warm water (110° to 115°)
1/2 cup molasses
2 tablespoons butter *or* margarine, softened
1 tablespoon aniseed, optional
1 tablespoon salt
5-1/2 to 6 cups all-purpose flour

In a bowl, pour boiling water over oats; let stand 30 minutes or until mixture has cooled to warm (110°-115°). In a large mixing bowl, dissolve yeast in warm water; let stand 5 minutes. Stir in oat mixture, molasses, butter, aniseed if desired, salt and 2 cups of flour; beat until smooth. Add enough remaining flour to form a soft dough. Turn onto a floured surface; knead until smooth and elastic, about 6-8 minutes. Place dough in a greased bowl, turning once to grease top. Cover and let rise in a warm place until doubled, about 1 hour. Punch dough down; divide in half. Shape into two loaves and place in greased 9-in. x 5-in. x 3-in. loaf pans. Cover and let rise until doubled, about 1 hour. Bake at 375° for 40 minutes or until bread sounds hollow when tapped. Remove from pans to cool on wire racks. **Yield:** 2 loaves. **If Cooking for Two:** Wrap one loaf in heavy-duty aluminum foil and freeze to enjoy later.

Quick & Easy

QUICK TOMATO/ STRAWBERRY SPREAD
Myra Innes, Auburn, Kansas

2 cups chopped peeled ripe tomatoes
1-1/2 cups sugar
1 package (3 ounces) strawberry-flavored gelatin

In a large kettle, bring tomatoes and sugar to a boil over medium-high heat, stirring often. Reduce heat; simmer for 15 minutes. Remove from the heat; stir in gelatin until dissolved. Cool for 10 minutes. Pour into jars or freezer containers, leaving 1/2-in. headspace. Top with lids. Let stand until set, up to 24 hours. Refrigerate or freeze. **Yield:** 2-2/3 cups.

WHETHER you prefer peaches and blueberries to raspberries or rhubarb...or favor jams and jellies to butters and preserves, here's the variety that suits any taste.

FRUIT AT ITS FINEST. Clockwise from lower left: **Honey Peach Butter**, **Cinnamon Blueberry Jam**, **Nutty Fruit Conserve**, **Raspberry Plum Jam**, **Heavenly Jam**, **Rhubarb Jelly**, **Tri-Berry Jam** and **Oven Apple Butter** (all recipes on pages 54 and 55).

HONEY PEACH BUTTER
Sharon Strube, Suwanee, Georgia
(PICTURED ON PAGE 52)

- 10 pounds peaches, peeled and chopped
- 1/2 cup water
- 4-1/2 cups sugar
- 1-1/2 cups honey

In a large kettle, cook the peaches in water until soft. Press through a sieve or food mill. Measure 12 cups pulp; return to kettle. Add sugar and honey. Cook, stirring often, until mixture thickens, about 1-1/4 hours. Stir more frequently as it thickens to prevent sticking. Pour hot into hot jars, leaving 1/4-in. headspace. Adjust caps. Process for 10 minutes in a boiling-water bath. **Yield:** 6 pints.

CINNAMON BLUEBERRY JAM
Barbara Burns, Phillipsburg, New Jersey
(PICTURED ON PAGE 52)

- 1 pound fresh *or* frozen blueberries (about 1 quart)
- 3-1/2 cups sugar
- 1 tablespoon lemon juice
- 1/4 teaspoon ground cinnamon
- 1/8 teaspoon ground cloves
- 1 pouch (3 ounces) liquid fruit pectin

Crush blueberries; measure 2-1/2 cups and place in a large kettle. Add the sugar, lemon juice, cinnamon and cloves; bring to a full rolling boil. Boil for 1 minute, stirring constantly. Stir in pectin; return to a full rolling boil. Boil for 1 minute, stirring constantly. Remove from heat. Skim off foam. Pour hot into hot jars, leaving 1/4-in. headspace. Adjust caps. Process 15 minutes in a boiling-water bath. **Yield:** 4 half-pints.

GARLIC LEMON BUTTER
Margie Wampler, Butler, Pennsylvania

- 1/2 cup butter *or* margarine, softened
- 1 garlic clove, minced
- 1 teaspoon minced fresh parsley
- 2 to 3 teaspoons grated lemon peel
- 1/4 teaspoon salt, optional
- Pepper to taste

In a small bowl, mix all ingredients until smooth. Spread on hot corn on the cob or dab on any cooked vegetables. **Yield:** 1/2 cup. **If Cooking for Two:** Lemon butter will keep in a covered container in the refrigerator for up to 2 weeks.

RASPBERRY PLUM JAM
Arlene Loker, Craigville, Indiana
(PICTURED ON PAGE 52)

- 4-1/2 cups chopped *or* coarsely ground pitted plums (about 2-1/2 pounds)
- 2 packages (10 ounces *each*) frozen raspberries in syrup, thawed
- 10 cups sugar
- 1/2 cup lemon juice
- 2 pouches (3 ounces *each*) liquid fruit pectin

In a large kettle, combine plums, raspberries, sugar and lemon juice. Bring to a full rolling boil over high heat, stirring constantly. Quickly stir in pectin; return to a full rolling boil. Boil for 1 minute, stirring constantly. Remove from the heat; skim off any foam. Pour hot into hot jars, leaving 1/4-in. headspace. Adjust caps. Process for 15 minutes in a boiling-water bath. **Yield:** 6 pints.

OVEN APPLE BUTTER
Virginia McNeese, Greenville, Illinois
(PICTURED ON PAGE 53)

- 40 large apples (about 13 pounds), quartered and cored
- 1/4 cup water
- 8 cups sugar
- 1 cup cider vinegar
- 4 teaspoons ground cinnamon
- 1 cinnamon stick (3 inches)

In a large covered kettle, simmer the apples and water until tender. Press through a sieve or food mill. Measure 1 gallon of pulp; place in a large heavy roaster. Add sugar, vinegar, cinnamon and cinnamon stick. Cover and bake at 400° for 3 hours, stirring occasionally. Uncover and bake 1 hour longer, stirring occasionally, until very thick. Remove cinnamon stick. Pour hot into hot jars, leaving 1/4-in. headspace. Adjust the caps. Process for 10 minutes in a boiling-water bath. **Yield:** 8 pints.

NUTTY FRUIT CONSERVE
Elfrieda Neufeld, Leamington, Ontario
(PICTURED ON PAGE 52)

- 5 cups chopped *or* coarsely ground peeled pears (about 4 pounds)
- 18 ounces dried apricots, coarsely ground
- 15 ounces golden raisins
- 3-1/2 cups sugar
- 1 teaspoon almond extract
- 1/2 teaspoon butter *or* margarine
- 8 ounces slivered almonds, coarsely chopped
- 1 pouch (3 ounces) liquid fruit pectin

In a large kettle, combine the first six ingredients. Cook and stir over medium heat until mixture thickens, about 20 minutes, adding the almonds during the last 5 minutes. Quickly stir in pectin. Bring to a full rolling boil and boil for 1 minute, stirring constantly. Remove from the heat; skim off any foam. Pour hot into hot jars, leaving 1/4-in. headspace. Remove air bubbles. Adjust caps. Process for 15 minutes in a boiling-water bath. **Yield:** 5 pints.

RHUBARB JELLY
Jean Coleman, Ottawa, Ontario
(PICTURED ON PAGE 53)

- 4-1/2 to 5 pounds rhubarb (4-1/2 to 5 quarts), cut into 1-inch pieces
- 7 cups sugar
- 1 to 2 drops red food coloring, optional
- 2 pouches (3 ounces *each*) liquid fruit pectin

Grind the rhubarb in a food processor or grinder. Strain through a jelly bag, reserving 3-1/2 cups of juice. Pour juice into a large kettle; add sugar and food coloring if desired. Bring to a boil over high heat, stirring constantly. Add pectin; bring to a full rolling boil. Boil for 1 minute, stirring constantly. Remove from the heat; let stand a few minutes. Skim off foam. Pour hot into hot jars, leaving 1/4-in. headspace. Adjust caps. Process for 10 minutes in a boiling-water bath. **Yield:** 8 half-pints.

MOM'S MUFFINS
Jane Jensen, Yuma, Arizona

- 2 cups all-purpose flour
- 2 tablespoons plus 1 teaspoon sugar

4 teaspoons baking powder
1 teaspoon salt
2 eggs, beaten
3/4 cup milk
1/4 cup vegetable oil

In a mixing bowl, combine flour, sugar, baking powder and salt. Make a well in the center. Combine eggs, milk and oil. Pour into well and mix just until dry ingredients are moistened (do not overmix). Spoon into greased muffin cups. Bake at 400° for 20-25 minutes or until golden brown. **Yield:** 1 dozen. **If Cooking for Two:** Freeze baked muffins in freezer bags; thaw and reheat as needed.

TRI-BERRY JAM
Karen Maerkle, Baltic, Connecticut
(PICTURED ON PAGE 53)

4 cups fresh *or* frozen
   blueberries
2-1/2 cups fresh *or* frozen red
   raspberries
2-1/2 cups fresh *or* frozen
   strawberries
1/4 cup lemon juice
2 packages (1-3/4 ounces
   each) powdered fruit pectin
11 cups sugar

Combine the berries and lemon juice in a large kettle; crush fruit slightly. Stir in pectin. Bring to a full rolling boil over high heat, stirring constantly. Stir in sugar; return to a full rolling boil. Boil 1 minute, stirring constantly. Remove from the heat; skim off any foam. Pour hot into hot jars, leaving 1/4-in. headspace. Adjust caps. Process for 15 minutes in a boiling-water bath. **Yield:** about 6 pints.

HEAVENLY JAM
Kathleen Bailey, Penetanguishene, Ontario
(PICTURED ON PAGE 53)

2 medium oranges
1 lemon
Pinch baking soda
6 medium pears
6 medium peaches
6 medium apples
Sugar

Grind unpeeled oranges and lemon in a food processor or grinder; transfer to a large kettle. Add baking soda; simmer for 10 minutes. Peel the remaining fruit; grind, then crush it. Add to orange mixture; measure and return to kettle. Add sugar equal to the amount of fruit. Boil until thick, about 30 minutes. Pour hot into hot jars, leaving 1/4-in. headspace. Adjust caps. Process for 20

minutes in a boiling-water bath. **Yield:** about 7 pints. **Editor's Note:** This recipe does not require pectin.

RHUBARB BLUEBERRY JAM
Dorothea Cleveland, Loveland, Colorado

5 cups diced fresh *or* frozen
   rhubarb
1 cup water
5 cups sugar
1 can (21 ounces) blueberry pie
   filling
1 package (6 ounces)
   raspberry-flavored gelatin

In a large kettle, combine rhubarb and water. Cook over medium-high heat for 4 minutes or until rhubarb is tender. Add sugar and bring to a boil. Boil for 2 minutes. Stir in pie filling. Remove from the heat; cool for 10 minutes. Add gelatin and mix well. Pour hot into hot jars, leaving 1/4-in. headspace. Adjust caps. Process for 15 minutes in a boiling-water bath. **Yield:** about 8 half-pints.

BREAD BIRDS
Iris Karl, Waynesboro, Virginia
(PICTURED BELOW)

3 to 3-1/2 cups bread flour
   (no substitutes), *divided*
1/4 cup sugar
1 package (1/4 ounce) active
   dry yeast

1 teaspoon salt
1/4 cup butter *or* margarine
1/2 cup milk
1/2 cup water
1/2 teaspoon almond extract
1 egg, lightly beaten
16 slivered almonds
32 currants
HONEY BUTTER:
1/4 cup butter *or* margarine,
   softened
2 tablespoons honey

In a large mixing bowl, combine 1 cup flour, sugar, yeast and salt. In a saucepan, melt butter. Add milk and water; heat to 120°-125°. Add to flour mixture and mix well. Stir in extract and egg; beat until smooth. Add enough remaining flour to form a soft dough. Turn onto a floured board; knead until smooth and elastic, about 6-8 minutes. Place in a greased bowl, turning once to grease top. Cover and let rise in a warm place until doubled, about 1 hour. Punch the dough down; divide into 16 pieces. To shape birds, roll each piece into a 10-in. rope; tie into a knot. Cut one end a few times with a scissors to form tail feathers. Tuck in the other end of the knot to form head. Place on a greased baking sheet. Cover and let rise until almost doubled, about 30 minutes. Bake at 350° for 17-20 minutes or until golden brown. Combine honey butter ingredients; brush over the hot rolls. Return to the oven for 3 minutes. With a toothpick, make small holes for the beak and eyes. Insert a slivered almond for the beak and currants for eyes. Serve with remaining honey butter if desired. **Yield:** 16 rolls.

YOUR family will thank you when they sample the bounty of brownies featured here. They're the very best—and most delicious—being made across the country.

RENOWNED BROWNIES. Clockwise from lower right: **Ultimate Double Chocolate Brownies**, **Swiss Chocolate Brownies**, **Raspberry Truffle Brownies** and **Chocolate Peanut Butter Brownies** (all recipes on page 57).

RECIPE

Cakes, Cookies & Bars

Cakes, cookies and bars are always on hand in any country cook's kitchen. And this superb selection will surely satisfy any sweet tooth.

ULTIMATE DOUBLE CHOCOLATE BROWNIES
Carol Prewett, Cheyenne, Wyoming
(PICTURED AT LEFT)

3/4 cup baking cocoa
1/2 teaspoon baking soda
2/3 cup butter *or* margarine, melted, *divided*
1/2 cup boiling water
2 cups sugar
2 eggs
1-1/3 cups all-purpose flour
1 teaspoon vanilla extract
1/4 teaspoon salt
1/2 cup coarsely chopped pecans
2 cups (12 ounces) semisweet chocolate chunks

In a large bowl, combine cocoa and baking soda; blend in 1/3 cup melted butter. Add boiling water; stir until well blended. Stir in sugar, eggs and remaining butter. Add flour, vanilla and salt. Stir in the pecans and chocolate chunks. Pour into a greased 13-in. x 9-in. x 2-in. baking pan. Bake at 350° for 35-40 minutes or until brownies begin to pull away from sides of pan. Cool. **Yield:** 3 dozen.

CHOCOLATE PEANUT BUTTER BROWNIES
Patsy Burgin, Lebanon, Indiana
(PICTURED AT LEFT)

2 squares (1 ounce *each*) unsweetened chocolate
1/2 cup butter *or* margarine
2 eggs
1 cup sugar
1/2 cup all-purpose flour
FILLING:
1-1/2 cups confectioners' sugar
1/2 cup creamy peanut butter
1/4 cup butter *or* margarine, softened
2 to 3 tablespoons light cream *or* milk
GLAZE:
1 square (1 ounce) semisweet baking chocolate
1 tablespoon butter *or* margarine

In a small saucepan, melt chocolate and butter over low heat; set aside. In a mixing bowl, beat eggs and sugar until light and pale colored. Add flour and melted chocolate; stir well. Pour into a greased 9-in. square baking pan. Bake at 350° for 25 minutes or until the brownies test done. Cool. For filling, beat confectioners' sugar, peanut butter and butter in a mixing bowl. Stir in cream or milk until mixture reaches desired spreading consistency. Spread over cooled brownies; cover and chill until firm. For glaze, melt chocolate and butter in a saucepan, stirring until smooth. Drizzle over the filling. Chill before cutting. Store in the refrigerator. **Yield:** about 5 dozen.

SWISS CHOCOLATE BROWNIES
Gloria Stange, Claresholm, Alberta
(PICTURED AT LEFT)

1 cup water
1/2 cup butter *or* margarine
1-1/2 squares (1-1/2 ounces) unsweetened chocolate
2 cups all-purpose flour
2 cups sugar
1 teaspoon baking soda
1/2 teaspoon salt
2 eggs, lightly beaten
1/2 cup sour cream
1/2 teaspoon vanilla extract
1 cup chopped walnuts
ICING:
1/2 cup butter *or* margarine
1-1/2 squares (1-1/2 ounces) unsweetened chocolate
3 cups confectioners' sugar, *divided*
5 tablespoons milk
1 teaspoon vanilla extract

In a saucepan, bring water, butter and chocolate to a boil. Boil for 1 minute. Remove from the heat; cool. In a mixing bowl, combine flour, sugar, baking soda and salt. Add chocolate mixture and mix. Add eggs, sour cream and

vanilla; mix. Fold in walnuts. Pour into a greased 15-in. x 10-in. x 1-in. baking pan. Bake at 350° for 20-25 minutes or until brownies test done. Cool for 10 minutes. For icing, melt butter and chocolate. Place in a mixing bowl; mix in 1-1/2 cups confectioners' sugar. Add milk, vanilla and remaining sugar; beat until smooth. Spread over warm brownies. **Yield:** about 3 dozen.

RASPBERRY TRUFFLE BROWNIES
Leslie Knicl, Mahomet, Illinois
(PICTURED AT LEFT)

1/2 cup butter *or* margarine
1-1/4 cups semisweet chocolate chips
2 eggs
3/4 cup packed brown sugar
1 teaspoon instant coffee crystals
2 tablespoons water
1/2 teaspoon baking powder
3/4 cup all-purpose flour
FILLING:
1 cup (6 ounces) semisweet chocolate chips
1 package (8 ounces) cream cheese, softened
1/4 cup confectioners' sugar
1/3 cup seedless red raspberry jam
GLAZE:
1/4 cup semisweet chocolate chips
1 teaspoon shortening

In a heavy saucepan, melt butter and chocolate chips over low heat. Cool slightly. In a large bowl, beat eggs and brown sugar. Dissolve coffee crystals in water; add to egg mixture with melted chocolate. Mix well. Combine baking powder and flour; stir into chocolate mixture. Spread in a greased 9-in. square baking pan. Bake at 350° for 30-35 minutes or until brownies test done. Cool. For filling, melt chocolate chips; cool. In a mixing bowl, beat cream cheese until fluffy; add confectioners' sugar and jam. Stir in melted chocolate; spread over cooled brownies. For glaze, melt chocolate chips and shortening. Drizzle over filling. Chill before cutting. Store in the refrigerator. **Yield:** about 5 dozen.

SPICED CHIFFON CAKE
Vera Woodward, Carmichael, California
(PICTURED AT RIGHT)

1-1/2 cups sugar
  2 cups all-purpose flour
  1 tablespoon baking powder
  1 teaspoon salt
  1 teaspoon ground cinnamon
1/2 teaspoon ground allspice
1/2 teaspoon ground cloves
1/2 teaspoon ground nutmeg
3/4 cup cold water
1/2 cup vegetable oil
  7 eggs, *separated*
1/2 teaspoon cream of tartar
GLAZE:
  2 tablespoons butter *or*
    margarine
  1 tablespoon all-purpose flour
1/8 teaspoon salt
1/4 cup milk
1/4 cup packed brown sugar
1/4 teaspoon vanilla extract
  1 cup confectioners' sugar
Chopped walnuts

In a large mixing bowl, combine sugar, flour, baking powder, salt, cinnamon, allspice, cloves and nutmeg. Add water, oil and egg yolks. Beat on low speed just until combined. Increase speed and beat until smooth. Set aside. Whip egg whites with cream of tartar until stiff peaks form; fold into batter. Pour into an ungreased 10-in. tube pan. Bake at 325° for 70 minutes or until top springs back when lightly touched. Immediately invert pan; cool completely. Remove cake from pan. For glaze, melt butter in a saucepan. Blend in flour and salt. Add milk all at once, stirring constantly. Bring to a boil; cook and stir until thick and bubbly. Remove from the heat; beat in brown sugar and vanilla. Add confectioners' sugar; mix until smooth. Drizzle over cake. Sprinkle with nuts. **Yield:** 12 servings.

COCONUT OAT COOKIES
Lou Ellen Planck, Flemingsburg, Kentucky

  1 cup butter *or* margarine,
    softened
  2 cups packed brown sugar
  1 teaspoon vanilla extract
  2 eggs
  2 cups all-purpose flour
  2 cups old-fashioned oats
  1 teaspoon baking powder
  1 teaspoon baking soda
  1 teaspoon salt
  2 cups flaked coconut
Pecan halves

In a mixing bowl, cream butter, brown sugar and vanilla. Add eggs, one at a time, beating well after each addition.

Combine flour, oats, baking powder, baking soda and salt; add to creamed mixture and mix well. Stir in coconut. Shape into 1-in. balls. Place 2-1/2 in. apart on greased baking sheets (cookies will spread). Place pecan half in the center of each cookie and push down slightly. Bake at 325° for 14-16 minutes. **Yield:** 4 dozen.

BANANA ORANGE BARS
Mary Sturgis, Hingham, Massachusetts

  2 cups mashed ripe bananas
    (3 to 4 bananas)
1-2/3 cups sugar
  1 cup vegetable oil
  4 eggs
  2 cups all-purpose flour
  2 teaspoons ground cinnamon
  2 teaspoons baking powder
  1 teaspoon baking soda
  1 teaspoon salt
ORANGE BUTTER FROSTING:
1/4 cup butter *or* margarine,
    softened
  3 cups confectioners' sugar
1/4 cup orange juice
1/2 teaspoon grated orange peel

In a mixing bowl, beat bananas, sugar, oil and eggs until well blended. Combine dry ingredients; fold into the banana mixture until well mixed. Pour into a greased 15-in. x 10-in. x 1-in. baking pan. Bake at 350° for 25-30 minutes; cool. For frosting, cream butter and sugar in a mixing bowl. Add orange juice and peel and beat until smooth. Spread over bars. **Yield:** 3 dozen.

SACHER TORTE COOKIES
Audrey Thibodeau, Fountain Hills, Arizona

  1 cup butter *or* margarine,
    softened
  1 package (3.9 ounces) instant
    chocolate pudding mix
  1 egg
  2 cups all-purpose flour
1/4 cup sugar
1/2 cup apricot, strawberry *or*
    raspberry preserves
GLAZE:
1/3 cup semisweet chocolate
    chips
  1 tablespoon butter *or*
    margarine

In a large mixing bowl, cream butter and pudding mix. Beat in egg; mix well. Stir in flour until thoroughly combined. Shape dough into 1-1/4-in. balls; roll in sugar. Place 2 in. apart on ungreased

baking sheets. Gently press thumb in the center of each ball to make an indentation. Bake at 325° for 15-18 minutes or until set. Cool a few minutes before removing from baking sheets; cool on wire rack. Fill indentations with preserves. For glaze, melt chocolate chips and butter in a small saucepan over very low heat, stirring constantly. Cool slightly. Drizzle over cookies. Cool completely. **Yield:** about 2-1/2 dozen.

MOLASSES CREAMS
Virginia Krites, Cridersville, Ohio

1-1/2 cups butter *or* margarine,
    softened
  2 cups sugar
  2 eggs, lightly beaten
1/2 cup light molasses
  4 cups all-purpose flour
  2 teaspoons baking soda
  1 teaspoon ground cinnamon
3/4 teaspoon ground ginger
1/2 teaspoon ground cloves
FROSTING:
1-1/2 cups confectioners' sugar
  3 tablespoons butter *or*
    margarine, softened
  1 tablespoon vanilla extract
  1 to 2 tablespoons milk

In a large mixing bowl, cream butter and sugar. Add eggs and molasses and mix thoroughly. Blend in dry ingredients. Roll into walnut-sized balls. Place on ungreased cookie sheets (do not flatten). Bake at 350° for 10-12 minutes or until done (centers will be slightly soft). In a small mixing bowl, beat frosting ingredients until creamy. Frost cookies while warm. **Yield:** about 8 dozen.

EASY COMPANY BARS
Ruby Lee Hughes, Lynchburg, Virginia

  2 tablespoons butter *or*
    margarine, melted
  2 eggs
  1 cup packed brown sugar
  1 teaspoon vanilla extract
1/3 cup all-purpose flour
1/8 teaspoon baking soda
  1 cup finely chopped nuts
Confectioners' sugar

Coat the bottom of an 8-in. square baking pan with melted butter. In a mixing bowl, beat eggs. Gradually beat in brown sugar and vanilla just until combined. Combine flour and baking soda; stir into the egg mixture. Fold in nuts. Pour batter evenly over butter; do not stir. Bake at 350° for 25 minutes or until bars test done with a toothpick. Cool slightly; dust with confectioners' sugar and cut. Cool completely. **Yield:** 1-1/2 dozen.

AT YOUR NEXT get-together, delight guests with easy-to-prepare pork roast. Everyone will love the old-fashioned flavors of fruit soup and brown bread. And for a sweet ending, try an eye-catching spice cake.

'TIS THE SEASON. Clockwise from top: **Spiced Chiffon Cake** (recipe on page 58), **Holiday Fruit Soup** (recipe on page 30), **New England Brown Bread** (recipe on page 50) and **Festive Pork Roast** (recipe on page 17).

SOUR CREAM RAISIN SQUARES
Leona Eash, McConnelsville, Ohio

1 cup butter *or* margarine, softened
1 cup packed brown sugar
2 cups all-purpose flour
2 cups quick-cooking oats
1 teaspoon baking powder
1 teaspoon baking soda
1/8 teaspoon salt
FILLING:
4 egg yolks
2 cups (16 ounces) sour cream
1-1/2 cups raisins
1 cup sugar
1 tablespoon cornstarch

In a mixing bowl, cream the butter and brown sugar. Beat in flour, oats, baking powder, baking soda and salt (mixture will be crumbly). Set aside 2 cups; pat remaining crumbs into a greased 13-in. x 9-in. x 2-in. baking pan. Bake at 350° for 15 minutes. Cool. Meanwhile, combine filling ingredients in a saucepan. Bring to a boil; cook and stir constantly for 5-8 minutes. Pour over crust; sprinkle with reserved crumbs. Return to the oven for 15 minutes. **Yield:** 12-16 servings.

PECAN TORTE
Joan Rice, De Soto, Texas
(PICTURED ON BACK COVER)

12 eggs, *separated*
2 cups sugar
2-1/2 cups ground pecans
1/2 cup dry bread crumbs
1/2 teaspoon vanilla extract
BUTTER CREAM FROSTING:
1 cup milk
1/4 cup cornstarch
2 cups (12 ounces) semisweet chocolate chips
1 cup butter (no substitutes), softened
2 cups confectioners' sugar
2 teaspoons vanilla extract
Whole pecans, optional

In a mixing bowl, beat egg yolks and sugar until thick and lemon-colored, about 5-6 minutes. Combine pecans and bread crumbs; stir into yolk mixture with vanilla. In another mixing bowl, beat the egg whites until stiff peaks form; fold into batter. Divide evenly among three greased and waxed paper-lined 9-in. round baking pans. Bake at 350° for 25-30 minutes or until cakes test done. Cool for 10 minutes before removing from pans; cool completely on a wire rack. For frosting, combine milk and cornstarch in a

saucepan until well blended. Add chocolate chips. Cook and stir over medium heat until thickened. Cool to room temperature. In a mixing bowl, cream butter and confectioners' sugar. Add vanilla and beat until smooth. Stir in chocolate mixture; beat until fluffy. Spread between cooled cake layers. Frost top and sides. Garnish with pecans if desired. **Yield:** 12-16 servings. **Editor's Note:** This is a rich, flourless torte.

CHEWY PECAN COOKIES
Janice Jackson, Haleyville, Alabama

1 cup butter *or* margarine, softened
1 cup sugar
3/4 cup packed brown sugar
3 eggs
1/4 cup milk
1 teaspoon vanilla extract
2-1/4 cups all-purpose flour
1 tablespoon ground cinnamon
1 teaspoon baking soda
1 teaspoon salt
1 teaspoon pumpkin pie *or* apple pie spice
2 cups quick-cooking oats
2 cups raisins
1-1/2 cups chopped pecans

In a large mixing bowl, beat butter, sugars, eggs, milk and vanilla. Combine dry ingredients; add to creamed mixture and mix well. Stir in oats, raisins and nuts; mix well. Drop by tablespoonfuls onto greased baking sheets. Bake at 350° for 10-12 minutes or until light golden brown. Remove from baking sheets to cool on wire racks. **Yield:** 5-6 dozen.

Quick & Easy

NO-BAKE PEANUT BROWNIES
Connie Ward, Mt. Pleasant, Iowa

4 cups graham cracker crumbs
1 cup chopped peanuts
1/2 cup confectioners' sugar
1/4 cup peanut butter
2 cups (12 ounces) semisweet chocolate chips
1 cup evaporated milk
1 teaspoon vanilla extract

Combine crumbs, peanuts, sugar and peanut butter using a whisk or pastry blender. In a small saucepan, melt the chocolate chips and milk over low heat, stirring constantly until smooth. Remove from the heat; add vanilla. Set aside 1/2 cup. Pour remaining chocolate mixture over crumb mixture and stir until well blended. Spread evenly in a greased 9-in. square baking pan. Frost with the reserved chocolate mixture. Chill for 1 hour. **Yield:** 2-1/2 dozen.

TRIPLE-LAYER BROWNIES
Cathy Slattery, Amsterdam, Missouri

1 cup quick-cooking oats
1/2 cup all-purpose flour
1/2 cup packed brown sugar
1/4 teaspoon baking soda
1/4 teaspoon salt
6 tablespoons butter *or* margarine, melted
MIDDLE LAYER:
3/4 cup sugar
1/4 cup butter *or* margarine, melted
1 square (1 ounce) unsweetened chocolate, melted
1 egg
1/2 teaspoon vanilla extract
2/3 cup all-purpose flour
1/4 teaspoon baking powder
1/4 teaspoon salt
1/4 cup milk
1/2 cup chopped pecans
FROSTING:
1 square (1 ounce) unsweetened chocolate
2 tablespoons butter *or* margarine
1-1/2 cups confectioners' sugar
1 teaspoon vanilla extract
Boiling water
16 pecan halves

In a bowl, combine the first five ingredients; stir in butter. Pat into a greased 11-in. x 7-in. x 2-in. baking pan. Bake at 350° for 5 minutes. In another bowl, combine sugar, butter and chocolate. Add egg and vanilla; mix well. Combine flour, baking powder and salt; add to the chocolate mixture alternately with milk. Stir in pecans; spread over bottom layer. Bake at 350° for 25 minutes. Cool. For frosting, melt chocolate and butter in a saucepan over low heat. Remove from the heat; stir in the confectioners' sugar and vanilla (mixture will be very crumbly). Beat in enough water (about 2 tablespoons) to achieve desired spreading consistency. Immediately frost brownies and top with pecan halves. **Yield:** 16 servings.

SUGARLESS BANANA WALNUT CAKE
Mildred Burkett, Greencastle, Pennsylvania

2/3 cup mashed bananas
1/2 cup butter *or* margarine, softened
3 eggs
2 cups all-purpose flour
2 teaspoons baking powder
1 teaspoon baking soda
1 teaspoon ground cinnamon
3/4 cup water
1 cup chopped walnuts

In mixing bowl, beat bananas and butter until creamy. Add eggs and beat well. Combine flour, baking powder, baking soda and cinnamon; add to banana mixture alternately with water, beating well after each addition. Stir in nuts. Spoon into a greased 9-in. square baking pan. Bake at 350° for 30 minutes or until cake tests done. Cool. **Yield:** 9 servings.

WALNUT GRAHAM TORTE
Paulette Root-Rogers
Red Feather Lakes, Colorado
(PICTURED ON FRONT COVER)

1 cup butter *or* margarine, softened
1 cup sugar
3 eggs, lightly beaten
2 cups graham cracker crumbs
1/2 cup all-purpose flour
1 teaspoon baking powder
1/2 teaspoon ground cinnamon
1/4 teaspoon salt
1 cup milk
2 cups diced peeled apples
1 cup chopped walnuts, *divided*
1-1/2 cups whipping cream
3 tablespoons confectioners' sugar

In a large mixing bowl, cream the butter and sugar. Add eggs; mix well. Combine graham cracker crumbs, flour, baking powder, cinnamon and salt; add to creamed mixture alternately with milk and mix well. Fold in apples and 3/4 cup walnuts. Spread into three greased 8-in. round cake pans. Bake at 350° for 25-30 minutes or until cakes test done. Cool for 10 minutes; remove from pans to wire racks to cool completely. Whip cream and confectioners' sugar until stiff; spread between layers and on top of torte. Sprinkle with remaining walnuts. **Yield:** 8-10 servings.

CARAMEL PUDDING CAKE
Lois Litalien, Bonners Ferry, Idaho

1/2 cup butter *or* margarine, softened
1/2 cup sugar
1-1/2 cups all-purpose flour
1 teaspoon baking powder
1/2 teaspoon salt
1/2 cup milk
1/2 cup raisins
1 cup packed brown sugar
2 cups cold water

In a mixing bowl, cream butter and sugar. Combine flour, baking powder and salt; add to creamed mixture with milk.

Stir until smooth. Stir in raisins. Spread in a greased 8-in. square baking pan. Combine brown sugar and cold water; pour over batter. Bake at 350° for 40 minutes or until golden brown. Serve warm. **Yield:** 9 servings.

Quick & Easy

PEANUT BUTTER BROWNIE CUPS
Karen Presbrey, Pascoag, Rhode Island

1 package (21-1/2 ounces) fudge brownie mix
15 to 18 miniature peanut butter cups

Mix brownie batter according to package directions. Fill paper-lined or foil-lined muffin cups two-thirds full. Remove wrappers from peanut butter cups; set one in each muffin cup and press down until batter meets the top edge of the candy. Bake at 350° for 20-25 minutes. **Yield:** about 1-1/2 dozen. **Editor's Note:** The Test Kitchen staff found Betty Crocker's Fudge Brownie mix bakes best for this recipe.

DATE NUT BARS
Margaret Asselin, Kimball, Michigan

2 cups sugar
2 cups all-purpose flour
2 teaspoons baking powder
1/4 teaspoon salt
2 cups chopped dates
2 cups chopped walnuts *or* pecans
4 eggs, lightly beaten
2 tablespoons butter *or* margarine, melted
1 teaspoon vanilla extract
Confectioners' sugar

In a large bowl, combine sugar, flour, baking powder, salt, dates and nuts. Add eggs, butter and vanilla; stir just until dry ingredients are moistened (batter will be very stiff). Spread in a greased 15-in. x 10-in. x 1-in. baking pan. Bake at 350° for 20-25 minutes or until golden brown. Cool bars on a wire rack. Dust with confectioners' sugar. **Yield:** 5 dozen. **If Cooking for Two:** Bars will keep well stored in airtight containers in the freezer.

BLARNEY STONES
Louise Kohr, Olympia, Washington

2 cups cake flour
2-1/4 teaspoons baking powder
3/4 teaspoon salt
1 cup heavy cream

1-1/2 cup confectioners' sugar
1/2 cup water
1 teaspoon almond extract *or* 1-1/2 teaspoons vanilla extract
3 egg whites, stiffly beaten
SNOW ICING:
2 cups confectioners' sugar
3 tablespoons light cream
Dash salt
2 teaspoons dry sherry, rum *or* cold coffee
Finely chopped peanuts

Combine flour, baking powder and salt; set aside. In a mixing bowl, whip cream until soft peaks form; gradually fold in sugar. Combine water and extract; add alternately with flour mixture to cream mixture, gently folding ingredients together after each addition just until combined. Fold in egg whites. Spread into a greased and waxed paper-lined 13-in. x 9-in. x 2-in. baking pan. Bake at 350° for 25-30 minutes or until cake tests done and is very lightly browned. Cool on a rack for 10 minutes. Remove from pan; cool completely. With fork, break cake into 1-1/4- to 1-1/2-in. pieces; set aside. For icing, mix sugar, cream, salt and sherry until smooth. If icing is too thin, add additional sugar; if it's too thick, stir in more cream. To frost, spear each cake cube with a fork; hold over bowl of icing and spoon icing over cake, coating all sides. Excess icing will drip back into bowl. Dip frosted cake cubes into peanuts; place on a wire rack. **Yield:** 6-7 dozen.

GRANDMOTHER'S CHOCOLATE CAKE
Gloria Edwards, McPherson, Kansas

1/2 cup butter *or* margarine, softened
1/2 cup sugar
1 cup packed brown sugar
2 eggs
1/2 cup milk
1 teaspoon vanilla extract
2 cups all-purpose flour
1/3 cup baking cocoa
1 teaspoon salt
1 teaspoon baking powder
1 teaspoon baking soda
1 cup boiling water
Confectioners' sugar, optional

In a large mixing bowl, cream butter and sugars. Add eggs, milk and vanilla; beat well. Combine flour, cocoa, salt, baking powder and soda; add to creamed mixture and mix well. Stir in water; mix until smooth. (Batter will be thin.) Pour into a greased and floured 13-in. x 9-in. x 2-in. baking pan. Bake at 350° for 35-40 minutes or until cake tests done. Cool on a wire rack. Dust with confectioners' sugar if desired. **Yield:** 12-16 servings.

NO ONE ever said brownies were boring...as this appealing assortment shows. When your hungry clan is asking for a sweet treat, try one of these recipes featuring fruit, nuts and, of course...chocolate!

CHOICE CHEWING. Clockwise from lower left: **Apricot Angel Brownies**, **German Chocolate Brownies**, **Chocolate Mint Brownies**, **Cinnamon Brownies**, **Maple Butterscotch Brownies**, **Chocolate Crunch Brownies**, **Black Forest Brownies** and **Chocolate Cream Cheese Brownies** (all recipes on pages 64 and 65).

BLACK FOREST BROWNIES
Toni Reeves, Medicine Hat, Alberta
(PICTURED ON PAGE 63)

1-1/3 cups all-purpose flour
1 teaspoon baking powder
1/2 teaspoon salt
1 cup butter *or* margarine
1 cup baking cocoa
4 eggs, beaten
2 cups sugar
1-1/2 teaspoons vanilla extract
1 teaspoon almond extract
1 cup chopped maraschino
    cherries
1/2 cup chopped nuts
ICING:
1/4 cup butter *or* margarine,
    softened
1 teaspoon vanilla extract
2 cups confectioners' sugar
6 tablespoons baking cocoa
1/4 cup milk
1/4 cup chopped nuts

Combine flour, baking powder and salt; set aside. In a large saucepan, melt butter. Remove from the heat and stir in cocoa until smooth. Blend in eggs, sugar and extracts. Stir in flour mixture, cherries and nuts. Pour into a greased 13-in. x 9-in. x 2-in. baking pan. Bake at 350° for 35 minutes or until brownies test done. For icing, blend butter, vanilla, sugar, cocoa and milk until smooth; spread over hot brownies. Sprinkle with nuts. Cool. **Yield:** 3 dozen.

CHOCOLATE CREAM CHEESE BROWNIES
Lisa Godfrey, Temple, Georgia
(PICTURED ON PAGE 62)

1 package (4 ounces) German
    sweet chocolate
3 tablespoons butter *or*
    margarine
2 eggs
3/4 cup sugar
1/2 cup all-purpose flour
1/2 teaspoon baking powder
1/4 teaspoon salt
1 teaspoon vanilla extract
1/4 teaspoon almond extract
1/2 cup chopped nuts
FILLING:
2 tablespoons butter *or*
    margarine
1 package (3 ounces) cream
    cheese, softened
1/4 cup sugar
1 egg
1 tablespoon all-purpose flour
1/2 teaspoon vanilla extract

In a saucepan, melt chocolate and butter over low heat, stirring frequently. Set aside. In a bowl, beat the eggs. Gradually add sugar, beating until thick. Combine flour, baking powder and salt; add to egg mixture. Stir in melted chocolate, extracts and nuts. Pour half of the batter into a greased 8-in. square baking pan; set aside. For filling, beat butter and cream cheese in a mixing bowl until light. Gradually add sugar, beating until fluffy. Blend in egg, flour and vanilla; mix well. Spread over batter in pan. Dollop remaining batter over filling. With a knife, cut through batter to create a marbled effect. Bake at 350° for 35-40 minutes or until brownies test done. Cool. Store in the refrigerator. **Yield:** about 2 dozen.

SAUCEPAN BROWNIES
Dorelene Doddridge, Kirk, Colorado

1 cup (6 ounces) semisweet
    chocolate chips
1/4 cup butter *or* margarine
2 cups biscuit mix
1 can (14 ounces) sweetened
    condensed milk
1 egg, lightly beaten
1 cup chopped walnuts

In a large saucepan, melt chocolate chips and butter over low heat. Stir until well blended; remove from the heat. Add biscuit mix, milk and egg; stir well until all lumps are gone. Add nuts. Pour into a greased 13-in. x 9-in. x 2-in. baking pan. Bake at 350° for 25 minutes. **Yield:** 2-1/2 dozen.

LAZY DAISY CAKE
Carrie Bartlett, Gallatin, Tennessee

2 eggs
1 cup sugar
1 teaspoon vanilla extract
1 cup cake flour
1 teaspoon baking powder
1/4 teaspoon salt
1/2 cup milk
2 tablespoons butter *or*
    margarine
FROSTING:
3/4 cup packed brown sugar
1/2 cup butter *or* margarine,
    melted
2 tablespoons light cream
1 cup shredded coconut

In a large mixing bowl, beat eggs, sugar and vanilla on high until thick and lemon-colored, about 4 minutes. Combine flour, baking powder and salt; add to egg mixture. Beat on low just until combined. Heat milk and butter in a small saucepan until butter melts. Add to batter; beat thoroughly (the batter

will be thin). Pour into a greased 9-in. square baking pan. Bake at 350° for 20-25 minutes or until cake tests done. Cool slightly. For frosting, blend all ingredients well; spread over warm cake. Broil about 4 in. from the heat for 3-4 minutes or until the top is lightly browned. **Yield:** 9 servings.

CHOCOLATE MINT BROWNIES
Helen Baines, Elkton, Maryland
(PICTURED ON PAGE 62)

1 cup all-purpose flour
1/2 cup butter *or* margarine,
    softened
1/2 teaspoon salt
4 eggs
1 teaspoon vanilla extract
1 can (16 ounces)
    chocolate-flavored syrup
1 cup sugar
FILLING:
2 cups confectioners' sugar
1/2 cup butter *or* margarine,
    softened
1 tablespoon water
1/2 teaspoon mint extract
3 drops green food coloring
TOPPING:
1 package (10 ounces) mint
    chocolate chips
9 tablespoons butter *or*
    margarine

Combine the first seven ingredients in a large mixing bowl; beat at medium speed for 3 minutes. Pour batter into a greased 13-in. x 9-in. x 2-in. baking pan. Bake at 350° for 30 minutes (top of brownies will still appear wet). Cool completely. Combine filling ingredients in a medium mixing bowl; beat until creamy. Spread over cooled brownies. Refrigerate until set. For topping, melt chocolate chips and butter over low heat in a small saucepan. Let cool for 30 minutes or until lukewarm, stirring occasionally. Spread over filling. Chill before cutting. Store in the refrigerator. **Yield:** 5-6 dozen.

MAPLE BUTTERSCOTCH BROWNIES
Grace Vonhold, Rochester, New York
(PICTURED ON PAGE 63)

1-1/2 cups packed brown sugar
1/2 cup butter *or* margarine,
    melted
1-1/2 teaspoons imitation maple
    flavoring
2 eggs

1-1/2 cups all-purpose flour
1 teaspoon baking powder
1 cup chopped walnuts
Confectioners' sugar, optional

In a bowl, combine brown sugar, butter and maple flavoring. Beat in the eggs, one at a time. Combine flour and baking powder; add to egg mixture. Stir in walnuts. Pour into a greased 9-in. square baking pan. Bake at 350° for 30 minutes or until brownies test done. Cool. Dust with confectioners' sugar if desired. **Yield:** 16 brownies.

APRICOT ANGEL BROWNIES
Tamara Sellman, Barrington, Illinois
(PICTURED ON PAGE 62)

2 bars (2 ounces *each*) white baking chocolate
1/3 cup butter *or* margarine
1/2 cup packed brown sugar
2 eggs, beaten
1/4 teaspoon vanilla extract
3/4 cup all-purpose flour
1/2 teaspoon baking powder
1/4 teaspoon salt
1 cup finely chopped dried apricots
1/4 cup sliced almonds
1/4 cup flaked coconut

In a saucepan, melt chocolate and butter over low heat, stirring constantly until all of the chocolate is melted. Remove from the heat; stir in brown sugar, eggs and vanilla until blended. Set aside. In a bowl, combine flour, baking powder and salt. Stir in chocolate mixture. Combine apricots, almonds and coconut; stir half into the batter. Pour into a greased 9-in. square baking pan. Sprinkle remaining apricot mixture on top. Bake at 350° for 25 minutes or until golden brown. Cool. **Yield:** about 2 dozen.

CINNAMON BROWNIES
Gail Mehle, Rock Springs, Wyoming
(PICTURED ON PAGE 63)

3/4 cup baking cocoa
1/2 teaspoon baking soda
2/3 cup butter *or* margarine, melted, *divided*
1/2 cup boiling water
2 cups sugar
2 eggs, beaten
1 teaspoon vanilla extract
1-1/3 cups all-purpose flour
1-1/2 to 2 teaspoons ground cinnamon
1/4 teaspoon salt
1 cup (6 ounces) semisweet chocolate chips

FROSTING:
6 tablespoons butter *or* margarine, softened
1/2 cup baking cocoa
2-2/3 cups confectioners' sugar
1 to 1-1/2 teaspoons ground cinnamon
1/3 cup evaporated milk
1 teaspoon vanilla extract

In a mixing bowl, combine cocoa and baking soda; blend in 1/3 cup melted butter. Add boiling water, stirring until thickened. Stir in sugar, eggs, vanilla and remaining butter. Add flour, cinnamon and salt. Fold in chocolate chips. Pour into a greased 13-in. x 9-in. x 2-in. baking pan. Bake at 350° for 40 minutes or until brownies test done. Cool. For frosting, cream butter in a mixing bowl. Combine cocoa, sugar and cinnamon; add alternately with the milk. Beat to a spreading consistency; add vanilla. Add more milk if necessary. Spread over the brownies. **Yield:** 3 dozen.

CHOCOLATE CRUNCH BROWNIES
Pat Mueller, Mitchell, South Dakota
(PICTURED ON PAGE 63)

1 cup butter *or* margarine, softened
2 cups sugar
4 eggs
6 tablespoons baking cocoa
1 cup all-purpose flour
2 teaspoons vanilla extract
1/2 teaspoon salt
1 jar (7 ounces) marshmallow creme
1 cup creamy peanut butter
2 cups (12 ounces) semisweet chocolate chips
3 cups crisp rice cereal

In a mixing bowl, cream butter and sugar; add eggs. Stir in cocoa, flour, vanilla and salt. Spread into a greased 13-in. x 9-in. x 2-in. baking pan. Bake at 350° for 25 minutes or until brownies test done. Cool. Spread marshmallow creme over cooled brownies. In a small saucepan, melt peanut butter and chocolate chips over low heat, stirring constantly. Remove from the heat; stir in the cereal. Spread over marshmallow layer. Chill before cutting. Store in the refrigerator. **Yield:** 3 dozen.

Quick & Easy

BREEZY BROWNIES
Mary Peterson, Centralia, Ontario

1 cup sugar
1/2 cup butter *or* margarine
4 eggs

1/8 teaspoon salt
3/4 cup chocolate syrup
1 cup plus 1 tablespoon all-purpose flour
1 cup chopped pecans

FROSTING:
1-1/2 cups sugar
6 tablespoons butter *or* margarine
1/3 cup milk
1/2 cup semisweet chocolate chips
1/2 cup chopped pecans

In a mixing bowl, cream sugar and butter. Add eggs and salt; beat well. Stir in chocolate syrup, flour and nuts. Pour into a greased 13-in. x 9-in. x 2-in. baking pan. Bake at 350° for 20 minutes. Cool for 15 minutes. For frosting, combine sugar, butter and milk in a saucepan. Bring to a boil, stirring frequently. Boil for 1 minute; remove from the heat and stir in chocolate chips until melted. Beat to spreading consistency, about 3 minutes. Add pecans; frost warm brownies. **Yield:** 2 dozen.

GERMAN CHOCOLATE BROWNIES
Karen Grimes, Stephens City, Virginia
(PICTURED ON PAGE 62)

1/2 cup butter *or* margarine
1 package (4 ounces) German sweet chocolate, broken into squares
1/2 cup sugar
1 teaspoon vanilla extract
2 eggs, lightly beaten
1 cup all-purpose flour
1/2 teaspoon baking powder
1/4 teaspoon salt
TOPPING:
2 tablespoons butter *or* margarine, melted
1/2 cup packed brown sugar
1 cup flaked coconut
1/2 cup chopped pecans
2 tablespoons corn syrup
2 tablespoons milk

In a saucepan, melt butter and chocolate, stirring until smooth. Cool slightly. Add sugar and vanilla; mix. Beat in the eggs. Mix in flour, baking powder and salt. Pour into a greased 9-in. square baking pan. Bake at 350° for 18-22 minutes or until brownies test done. For topping, combine butter and brown sugar in a bowl. Add coconut, pecans, corn syrup and milk; mix well. Drop by teaspoonfuls onto warm brownies; spread evenly. Broil several inches from the heat for 2-4 minutes or until top is browned and bubbly. **Yield:** 16 brownies.

HOP INTO the season of spring with this pretty appealing menu using fresh produce, leftover ham and decorative sugar cookies. It's a great way to brighten your day.

EASTER ENTREES. Clockwise from the top: **Grandma's Sugar Cookies** (recipe on page 67), **Asparagus-Stuffed Potatoes** (recipe on page 39) and **Pineapple Ham Loaf** (recipe on page 11).

ALMOND TEA CAKES
Janet Fennema Ringelberg, Troy, Ontario

2 cups butter *or* margarine
3/4 cup sugar
3/4 cup packed brown sugar
2 eggs
4 teaspoons almond extract
4 cups all-purpose flour
1 teaspoon baking powder
FILLING:
1 egg white
1/2 cup sugar
1/2 cup ground almonds
1/2 teaspoon lemon juice
Milk
Sliced almonds

In a mixing bowl, cream butter and sugars. Add eggs and extract; mix well. Add flour and baking powder (dough will be soft). Chill. For filling, stir egg white, sugar, almonds and lemon juice in a small bowl. Remove a portion of the dough at a time from the refrigerator. Place 1-in. balls of dough into miniature muffin cups, pressing slightly into sides and bottom. Place 1/2 teaspoon of filling into each. Cover with quarter-sized circles of dough. Brush with a little milk and top with an almond. Bake at 350° for 20-25 minutes or until golden. **Yield:** about 5 dozen.

LEMON RAISIN FILLED COOKIES
Nancy Johnson, Milton, Pennsylvania

1 cup shortening
2 cups packed brown sugar
3 eggs
4 cups all-purpose flour
1 teaspoon baking soda
1/2 teaspoon salt
FILLING:
1 cup sugar
2 tablespoons cornstarch
1 cup water
1 cup raisins
1 egg, beaten
1 tablespoon butter *or* margarine
3 tablespoons lemon juice
1 to 2 teaspoons finely grated lemon peel

In a mixing bowl, cream shortening and brown sugar. Add eggs, one at a time, beating well after each addition. Combine flour, baking soda and salt; add to creamed mixture and mix well. Cover and chill overnight. For filling, combine sugar and cornstarch in a saucepan. Add water; stir to dissolve. Add raisins; cook and stir until thickened and bubbly. Cook and stir 2 minutes more. Remove from the heat. Stir a little of the hot mixture into beaten egg; return all to saucepan. Bring to a gentle boil; cook and stir for 2 minutes. Remove from the heat; stir in butter, lemon juice and peel. Cool. Divide chilled dough into thirds. Roll out a portion at a time on a lightly floured board to 1/8-in. thickness. Cut into 2-1/2-in. circles. Place 1 teaspoon filling on half of the circles; top with remaining circles. Pinch edges together to seal; place on greased baking sheets. Bake at 375° for 12 minutes or until lightly browned. (Use any leftover filling in tarts or as a dessert sauce over cake.) **Yield:** about 4 dozen. **If Cooking for Two:** Freeze cookies in airtight containers or freezer bags; thaw as needed.

GRANDMA'S SUGAR COOKIES
Kristy Deloach, Baton Rouge, Louisiana
(PICTURED AT LEFT)

2 cups sugar
1 cup butter (no substitutes)
1 teaspoon vanilla extract
1/2 teaspoon salt
2 eggs, lightly beaten
2-2/3 cups all-purpose flour
2 teaspoons baking powder
3/4 teaspoon baking soda

In a mixing bowl, cream sugar, butter, vanilla and salt. Add eggs and mix well. Combine flour, baking powder and baking soda; add to creamed mixture. Chill until firm, about 1 hour. On a floured surface, roll dough to 1/4-in. thickness. Cut with a 2-1/2-in. cookie cutter; place on greased baking sheets. Bake at 375° for 7-8 minutes or until light golden brown. Decorate if desired. **Yield:** 6 dozen.

 Quick & Easy

ANGEL FOOD ICE CREAM CAKE
Madelon Howland, Sterling, New York

 This tasty dish uses less sugar, salt and fat. Recipe includes *Diabetic Exchanges.*

1 angel food cake (8 inches)
1/2 gallon vanilla ice cream, slightly softened
2 quarts fresh strawberries
Sugar *or* sugar substitute to taste

Cut the cake in half; tear one half into small pieces and set aside. Cut the other half into 12-14 thin slices; arrange in the bottom of a waxed paper-lined 13-in. x 9-in. x 2-in. baking pan, overlapping as needed. Spread softened ice cream over cake, pressing down to smooth. Gently press the small cake pieces into ice cream. Cover and freeze. Just before serving, slice strawberries and sweeten to taste. Cut dessert into squares and top with strawberries. **Yield:** 15 servings. **Diabetic Exchanges:** One serving (prepared with sugar-free ice cream and sugar substitute) equals 1-1/2 starch, 1 fat, 1/2 fruit; also, 183 calories, 131 mg sodium, 15 mg cholesterol, 34 gm carbohydrate, 6 gm protein, 4 gm fat.

 Quick & Easy

ONE-BOWL BROWNIES
Cheryl Smith, Hart, Texas

1 cup butter *or* margarine
2 cups sugar
4 eggs
1 teaspoon vanilla extract
6 tablespoons baking cocoa
2 cups all-purpose flour
Pinch salt
1/2 cup chopped nuts

In a mixing bowl, cream butter and sugar. Beat in eggs and vanilla. Combine cocoa, flour and salt; stir into creamed mixture. Add nuts. Pour into a greased 13-in. x 9-in. x 2-in. baking pan. Bake at 375° for 20-25 minutes. **Yield:** 2-1/2 dozen.

> **SUGAR SWAP.** For a rich caramel flavor in brownies, substitute brown sugar for granulated sugar.

CHRISTMAS MOLASSES COOKIES
Deborah Hill, Coffeyville, Kansas

3/4 cup sugar
2/3 cup butter *or* margarine, softened
1/4 cup orange juice
1/2 cup dark corn syrup
1/2 cup dark molasses
4-1/2 cups all-purpose flour
3/4 cup whole wheat flour
2 teaspoons ground ginger
1 teaspoon baking soda
1 teaspoon salt
1/2 teaspoon ground cloves
1/2 teaspoon ground nutmeg
1/2 teaspoon ground allspice

In a mixing bowl, cream sugar and butter. Blend in orange juice, corn syrup and molasses. Combine dry ingredients; add to creamed mixture and mix well. Chill 3-4 hours or overnight. Roll dough, a portion at a time, on a lightly floured surface to 1/4-in. thickness. Cut into desired shapes. Place 2 in. apart on greased baking sheets. Bake at 350° for 12-14 minutes. Cookies will be soft and chewy if baked 12 minutes; crunchy if baked longer. **Yield:** 6-7 dozen (2-1/2-inch cookies).

CAN ANYTHING compare with a country pie? In most families, the answer to that question is a resounding "No!" And that's likely to be doubly so with yours after they dig into these pleasing pies.

PRIZED PIES. Clockwise from top: **Coconut/Banana Cream Pie**, **German Chocolate Pie**, **Strawberry Lovers' Pie** and **Apple Cranberry Pie** (all recipes on page 69).

Pies & Desserts

*Family and friends will surely save room for dessert
when they know you're preparing one of these delicious recipes.
They're the fantastic finale to your favorite meal.*

GERMAN CHOCOLATE PIE
Cheryl Jacobson, Chino Valley, Arizona
(PICTURED AT LEFT)

   1 package (4 ounces) German
     chocolate
1/4 cup butter *or* margarine
   1 can (12 ounces) evaporated
     milk
1-1/2 cups sugar
   3 tablespoons cornstarch
1/8 teaspoon salt
   2 eggs, lightly beaten
   1 teaspoon vanilla extract
   1 unbaked deep-dish pastry
     shell (9 inches)
1/2 cup chopped pecans
1-1/3 cups flaked coconut

In a saucepan, melt chocolate and butter over low heat, stirring to mix well. Remove from the heat and gradually blend in milk; set aside. In a bowl, combine sugar, cornstarch and salt. Stir in eggs and vanilla. Gradually stir in chocolate mixture. Pour into pastry shell. Combine pecans and coconut; sprinkle over filling. Bake at 375° for 45-50 minutes or until puffed and browned. Cool 4 hours. Chill (filling will become firm as it cools). **Yield:** 6-8 servings.

APPLE CRANBERRY PIE
Janet Morgan-Cavallaro, Pincourt, Quebec
(PICTURED AT LEFT)

   2 cups fresh *or* frozen
     cranberries
1-3/4 cups sugar
1/3 cup quick-cooking tapioca
1/4 cup water
   2 teaspoons grated orange peel
   3 cups sliced peeled baking
     apples
Pastry for double-crust pie (9 inches)
   1 egg white, beaten
   1 tablespoon water
Additional sugar

In a saucepan, combine the cranberries, sugar, tapioca, water and orange peel. Bring to a boil, stirring occasionally. Remove from the heat and stir in apples. Set saucepan in a pan of cold water for 10 minutes, stirring occasionally. Mean-

while, line pie plate with the bottom pastry. Pour filling into crust. Top with remaining pastry or a lattice crust. If using a full top crust, cut a few slits in it. Beat egg white and water until foamy; brush over top pastry. Sprinkle with sugar. Bake at 375° for 45-55 minutes or until crust is golden brown and filling is bubbly. Cool completely. **Yield:** 6-8 servings.

  Quick & Easy

PUMPKIN CHIFFON PIE
Karen Grimes, Stephens City, Virginia

   1 package (3 ounces) cream
     cheese, softened
   1 tablespoon sugar
   1 carton (4 ounces) frozen
     whipped topping, thawed
     (1-1/2 cups)
   1 graham cracker crust
     (8 *or* 9 inches)
   1 cup cold milk
   2 packages (3.4 ounces *each*)
     instant vanilla pudding mix
   1 can (16 ounces) pumpkin
   1 teaspoon ground cinnamon
1/2 teaspoon ground ginger
1/4 teaspoon ground cloves
Chopped nuts *and/or* additional
   whipped topping, optional

In a mixing bowl, beat cream cheese and sugar until smooth. Add whipped topping and mix well. Spread into crust. In another bowl, beat milk and pudding mixes on low speed until combined; beat on high for 2 minutes. Let stand 3 minutes. Stir in pumpkin and spices; mix well. Spread over cream cheese layer. Chill. Garnish with nuts and/or whipped topping if desired. **Yield:** 6-8 servings.

STRAWBERRY LOVERS' PIE
Lauretha Rowe, Scranton, Kansas
(PICTURED AT LEFT)

   3 squares (1 ounce *each*)
     semisweet chocolate, *divided*
   1 tablespoon butter *or* margarine
   1 pastry shell (9 inches), baked
   2 packages (3 ounces *each*)
     cream cheese, softened
1/2 cup sour cream

   3 tablespoons sugar
1/2 teaspoon vanilla extract
   3 to 4 cups fresh strawberries,
     hulled
1/3 cup strawberry jam, melted

In a saucepan, melt 2 ounces chocolate and butter over low heat, stirring constantly; spread or brush over the bottom and up the sides of pastry shell. Chill. Meanwhile, in a mixing bowl, beat cream cheese, sour cream, sugar and vanilla until smooth. Spread over chocolate layer; cover and chill for 2 hours. Arrange strawberries, tip end up, atop the filling. Brush jam over strawberries. Melt the remaining chocolate and drizzle over all. **Yield:** 6-8 servings.

COCONUT/BANANA
CREAM PIE
Tammy Olson, Bruce, South Dakota
(PICTURED AT LEFT)

CRUST:
   3 cups flaked coconut
   7 tablespoons butter *or*
     margarine
FILLING:
3/4 cup sugar
1/4 cup all-purpose flour
   3 tablespoons cornstarch
1/4 teaspoon salt
   3 cups light cream
   4 egg yolks, lightly beaten
   2 teaspoons vanilla extract
   2 large firm bananas, sliced
Whipped cream and sliced bananas,
   optional

In a skillet, saute coconut in butter until golden. Press all but 2 tablespoons into the bottom and up the sides of a greased 9-in. pie plate. Bake at 350° for 7 minutes. In a saucepan, combine the sugar, flour, cornstarch and salt. Gradually add cream and bring to a boil. Cook and stir constantly for 2 minutes. Add a small amount to egg yolks. Return all to pan; cook for 2 minutes. Remove from heat; add vanilla. Cool to room temperature. Place bananas in the crust. Cover with cream mixture. Chill until set, about 2 hours. Sprinkle with reserved coconut. If desired, garnish with whipped cream and bananas. **Yield:** 6-8 servings.

GERMAN APPLE PIE
Mrs. Woodrow Taylor, Adams Center, New York
(PICTURED AT RIGHT)

CRUST:
1-1/2 cups all-purpose flour
1/2 teaspoon salt
1/2 cup shortening
1 teaspoon vanilla extract
2 to 3 tablespoons ice water
FILLING:
1 cup sugar
1/4 cup all-purpose flour
2 teaspoons ground cinnamon
6 cups sliced peeled baking
apples
1 cup heavy cream
Whipped cream, optional

In a bowl, combine flour and salt; cut in shortening until the mixture resembles coarse crumbs. Sprinkle with vanilla and stir in. Sprinkle with water, 1 tablespoon at a time, stirring until pastry holds together. Shape into a ball. On a lightly floured surface, roll the dough to 1/8-in. thickness. Transfer to a 9-in. pie plate; trim and flute edges. For filling, combine sugar, flour and cinnamon; sprinkle 3 tablespoons into crust. Top with half of the apples. Sprinkle with half of the remaining sugar mixture. Top with remaining apples and sugar mixture. Pour cream over all. Bake at 450° for 10 minutes. Reduce heat to 350°; bake for 55-60 minutes or until apples are tender. Cool. Serve with whipped cream if desired. **Yield:** 6-8 servings.

DAIRY STATE APPLE PIE
Ethel Mueller, Chilton, Wisconsin
(PICTURED AT RIGHT)

CRUST:
1 cup all-purpose flour
5 tablespoons butter *or*
margarine
1/2 cup shredded cheddar cheese
1/2 teaspoon salt
3 to 4 tablespoons milk
FILLING:
1 package (3 ounces) cream
cheese, softened
1 egg
1/2 cup sugar
5 cups sliced peeled baking
apples
TOPPING:
1/4 cup all-purpose flour
1/4 cup sugar
1/4 teaspoon ground cinnamon
2 tablespoons butter *or*
margarine
1/4 cup chopped walnuts *or*
hickory nuts
Vanilla ice cream, optional

In a bowl, stir flour, butter, cheese and salt until crumbly. Sprinkle with milk, 1 tablespoon at a time, stirring until pastry holds together; form into a ball. Roll out on a lightly floured board. Transfer to a 9-in. pie pan; trim and flute edges. In a mixing bowl, beat cream cheese, egg and sugar until smooth. Stir in apples; pour into crust. In another bowl, mix flour, sugar and cinnamon. Cut in butter until crumbly. Stir in nuts. Sprinkle over apples. Bake at 350° for 15 minutes. Reduce heat to 300°; bake for 30-35 minutes or until apples are tender. Serve warm or chilled with ice cream if desired. **Yield:** 8 servings.

CREAMY PEACH PIE
Eva Thiessen, Cecil Lake, British Columbia

1 package (3 ounces)
peach-flavored gelatin
2/3 cup boiling water
1 cup vanilla ice cream
1 carton (8 ounces) frozen
whipped topping, thawed
1 cup diced peeled fresh
peaches
1 deep-dish pastry shell
(9 inches), baked
Sliced peaches *and/or* mint leaves,
optional

In a large bowl, dissolve gelatin in boiling water; stir in ice cream until melted and smooth. Add whipped topping and mix well. Fold in peaches. Pour into pastry shell. Chill until firm, about 3 hours. If desired, garnish with peaches and/or mint leaves. **Yield:** 6-8 servings.

PRALINE PEACH COBBLER
Maithel Martin, Kansas City, Missouri

1-1/2 cups plus 2 teaspoons sugar,
divided
2 tablespoons cornstarch
1 teaspoon ground cinnamon
1 cup water
8 cups sliced peeled fresh
peaches
2 cups self-rising flour*
1/2 cup shortening
1/2 cup buttermilk
3 tablespoons butter *or*
margarine, melted
1/4 cup packed brown sugar
1 cup chopped pecans

In a saucepan, mix 1-1/2 cups sugar, cornstarch, cinnamon and water; stir until smooth. Add peaches; cook and stir until thickened and bubbly. Cook and stir for 2 minutes more. Pour into a lightly greased 13-in. x 9-in. x 2-in. baking dish; set aside. In a bowl, combine flour and remaining sugar; cut in short-ening until mixture resembles coarse crumbs. Add buttermilk and stir just until moistened. If needed, add additional buttermilk, 1 tablespoon at a time, until dough clings together. Turn onto a floured surface; knead gently 6-8 times. Roll into a 12-in. x 8-in. rectangle. Combine butter, brown sugar and pecans; spread over the dough to within 1/2 in. of edges. Starting with long side, roll up jelly-roll style. Cut into 12 pieces, 1 in. each. Place on top of the peach mixture. Bake at 400° for 25-30 minutes or until golden brown. **Yield:** 12 servings. (*If self-rising flour is not available, substitute 2 cups all-purpose flour, 1 tablespoon baking powder and 1 teaspoon salt.)

SOUTHERN SWEET POTATO PIE
Bonnie Holcomb, Fulton, Mississippi

3 tablespoons all-purpose flour
1-2/3 cups sugar
1 cup mashed sweet potatoes
2 eggs
1/4 cup light corn syrup
1/4 teaspoon ground nutmeg
Pinch salt
1/2 cup butter *or* margarine
3/4 cup evaporated milk
1 unbaked pastry shell
(9 inches)

In a large mixing bowl, combine the flour and sugar. Add potatoes, eggs, corn syrup, nutmeg, salt, butter and evaporated milk; beat well. Pour into pastry shell. Bake at 350° for 55-60 minutes. **Yield:** 8 servings.

Quick & Easy

CHOCOLATE PEANUT BUTTER PIE
Carole Taylor, Mason City, Iowa

1 package (3.9 ounces) instant
chocolate pudding mix
1-3/4 cups cold milk
1 chocolate cookie crust
(8 *or* 9 inches)
2 cups whipped topping
4 peanut butter cups (.6 ounce
each), coarsely chopped

In a mixing bowl, beat pudding mix and milk on low speed until combined; beat for 2 minutes on high. Pour into crust. Chill for 20 minutes or until filling is thickened. Cover with the whipped topping. Sprinkle peanut butter cups on top. Chill. **Yield:** 6-8 servings.

YOU'LL HARVEST a bushel of smiles when you serve these winning recipes. No one can resist the garden-fresh goodness of apples, tomatoes, green peppers and onions.

APPLE OF YOUR EYE. Clockwise from bottom left: **Meatball Sandwiches** (recipe on page 11), **Dairy State Apple Pie** (recipe on page 70), **Cherry Tomato Salad** (recipe on page 35) and **German Apple Pie** (recipe on page 70).

BLUEBERRY PINEAPPLE CREAM

Sue Anna Schmucker, Dalton, Wisconsin

    1 cup graham cracker crumbs
    1/3 cup sugar
    1/3 cup butter *or* margarine,
        melted
    1 can (8 ounces) crushed
        pineapple
    30 large marshmallows
    2 packages (8 ounces *each*)
        cream cheese, softened
    1 carton (8 ounces) frozen
        whipped topping, thawed
    1 can (21 ounces) blueberry pie
        filling
**Additional graham cracker crumbs,
    optional**

In a bowl, combine the graham cracker crumbs, sugar and butter. Press into the bottom of a 13-in. x 9-in. x 2-in. baking pan. Bake at 350° for 10 minutes. Cool completely. Meanwhile, drain the pineapple juice into a saucepan; set pineapple aside. Add marshmallows to juice; cook and stir until melted. Remove from the heat and cool for 10 minutes. In a mixing bowl, beat cream cheese until smooth. Add marshmallow mixture; beat well. Fold in the pineapple and whipped topping; spread half over crust. Cover with pie filling. Chill for 30 minutes. Top with the remaining cream cheese mixture. Sprinkle with additional graham cracker crumbs if desired. Chill for 30 minutes. Store in the refrigerator. **Yield: 12-16 servings.**

"MOCK" SOUR CREAM RAISIN PIE

Danile Keily-Zent, Yakima, Washington

 This tasty dish uses less sugar, salt and fat. Recipe includes *Diabetic Exchanges*.

    1 cup skim milk
    1 carton (8 ounces) plain yogurt
    1 package (.8 ounce) sugar-free
        cook-and-serve vanilla
        pudding mix
    1/2 teaspoon ground allspice
    3/4 cup raisins
    1 pastry shell (9 inches), baked
**Light frozen whipped topping,
    thawed, optional**

In a saucepan, combine milk and yogurt. Add the pudding mix; cook and stir constantly until mixture boils and thickens. Stir in allspice. Add raisins; mix well and let cool for 10 minutes, stirring occasionally. Pour into pastry shell. Chill at least 2 hours. Serve with whipped topping if desired. **Yield: 8 servings. Dia-**

---

betic Exchanges: One serving (without whipped topping) equals 1-1/2 fat, 1 fruit, 1/2 skim milk; also, 175 calories, 210 mg sodium, 1 mg cholesterol, 24 gm carbohydrate, 4 gm protein, 8 gm fat.

FRESH FRUIT COBBLER

Paula Chick, Lewiston, Maine
(PICTURED ON PAGE 22)

    5 to 6 cups chopped
        fresh fruit (apples, rhubarb,
        blueberries *or* peaches)*
    2 cups all-purpose flour
    1/2 cup sugar
    4 teaspoons baking powder
    1 teaspoon salt
    1/2 cup butter *or* margarine
    1 cup milk
TOPPING:
    2/3 cup sugar
    1/4 cup cornstarch
    1-1/2 cups boiling water

Arrange fruit evenly in the bottom of a 13-in. x 9-in. x 2-in. greased baking pan. In a bowl, combine flour, sugar, baking powder and salt; cut in butter until crumbly. Stir in milk. Spoon over fruit. Combine sugar and cornstarch; sprinkle over batter. Pour water over all. Bake at 350° for 40-45 minutes or until fruit is tender. **Yield: 12-16 servings. *Editor's Note:** If desired, a combination of apples and rhubarb or blueberries and peaches can be used.

PUMPKIN PECAN PIE

Linda Frew, Cooper, Texas
(PICTURED ON PAGE 9)

    3/4 cup packed brown sugar
    1/2 teaspoon ground cinnamon
    1/4 teaspoon salt
    1 cup canned *or* cooked
        pumpkin
    3 eggs, lightly beaten
    1/2 cup dark corn syrup
    1 teaspoon vanilla extract
    1 unbaked pastry shell
        (9 inches)
    3/4 cup coarsely chopped pecans
**About 20 pecan halves
Whipped cream, optional**

In a large mixing bowl, combine brown sugar, cinnamon and salt. Add pumpkin, eggs, corn syrup and vanilla; beat well. Pour into the pastry shell. Sprinkle with chopped pecans. Place pecan halves around the outer edge of filling. Bake at 425° for 15 minutes. Reduce the heat to 350°; bake 25 more minutes or until a knife inserted near the center comes out clean. Cool. Serve with whipped cream if desired. **Yield: 6-8 servings.**

RHUBARB CRUNCH

Esther Mishler, Hollsopple, Pennsylvania

    1 cup all-purpose flour
    3/4 cup rolled oats
    1 cup packed brown sugar
    1 teaspoon ground cinnamon
    1/2 cup butter *or* margarine,
        melted
    4 cups sliced fresh *or* frozen
        rhubarb
TOPPING:
    1 cup sugar
    2 tablespoons cornstarch
    1 cup water
    1 teaspoon vanilla extract
**Few drops red food coloring,
    optional**

In a large bowl, combine flour, oats, brown sugar, cinnamon and butter; mix until crumbly. Press half of the mixture into an ungreased 9-in. square baking pan. Cover with rhubarb. For topping, combine sugar and cornstarch in a small saucepan; add water. Cook and stir until thickened and bubbly. Cook and stir 2 minutes more. Remove from the heat. Stir in vanilla and food coloring if desired. Pour over the rhubarb. Top with the remaining crumb mixture. Bake at 350° for 50-60 minutes or until bubbly. **Yield: 8-10 servings.**

CHERRY-LEMON ICEBOX PIE

Mary Weller, Twin Lake, Michigan

    1 can (14 ounces) sweetened
        condensed milk
    1/2 cup lemon juice
    1/2 teaspoon vanilla extract
    1/2 teaspoon almond extract
    1/2 cup heavy cream
    1 pastry shell (9 inches), baked
    1 can (21 ounces) cherry pie
        filling

In a bowl, combine the milk, lemon juice and extracts; stir until thickened, about 2 minutes. Beat cream until stiff; fold into milk mixture. Pour into pastry shell. Refrigerate for 10 minutes; top with pie filling. Chill for at least 2 hours or overnight if desired. **Yield: 6-8 servings.**

CRANBERRY BETTY

Leona Cullen, Melrose, Massachusetts

    4 cups soft bread crumbs
    6 tablespoons butter *or*
        margarine, *divided*
    5 cups sliced peeled baking
        apples (4 to 5 large)
    1 cup packed brown sugar

3/4 teaspoon ground nutmeg
2 cups fresh *or* frozen
cranberries
LEMON SAUCE:
1/2 cup sugar
1 tablespoon cornstarch
Pinch salt
1 cup water
1 teaspoon grated lemon peel
2 tablespoons lemon juice
2 tablespoons butter *or*
margarine

In a skillet, brown the bread crumbs in 3 tablespoons butter. Place half the apples in a greased 8-in. square baking dish. Combine the brown sugar and nutmeg; sprinkle half over apples. Top with half of the bread crumbs. Dot with half of the remaining butter. Place the cranberries on top. Layer with remaining apples, brown sugar mixture, bread crumbs and butter. Cover and bake at 350° for 45 minutes. Uncover and bake 15-20 minutes more or until fruit is tender. For lemon sauce, combine sugar, cornstarch and salt in a saucepan; add water and lemon peel. Bring to a boil; cook 2 minutes or until thick. Remove from the heat; stir in lemon juice and butter until melted. Serve over warm Cranberry Betty. **Yield:** 6-8 servings.

DAD'S PEACH ICE CREAM
Thelma Waggoner, Hopkinsville, Kentucky
(PICTURED ON PAGE 29)

4 cups milk
2-1/2 cups sugar
1/4 teaspoon salt
4 eggs, beaten
5 cups heavy cream
2 cups pureed peaches *or*
nectarines
1 tablespoon vanilla extract
1/4 to 1/2 teaspoon almond extract, optional

In heavy saucepan, heat milk over low until hot but not boiling. Stir in sugar and salt until dissolved. Gradually stir a quarter of the hot mixture into eggs, mixing constantly. Return all to the saucepan, stirring constantly. Continue to cook and stir for 10-12 minutes or until mixture coats the back of a metal spoon. Remove from the heat; cool. Chill for at least 2 hours or overnight. In a large bowl, combine the cream, fruit, vanilla and almond extract if desired. Add the chilled milk mixture, stirring well. Pour into a chilled freezer can of a 1-gallon ice cream freezer. Freeze according to manufacturer's instructions. **Yield:** 3 quarts. **Editor's Note:** For vanilla ice cream, add an additional 2 teaspoons of vanilla extract and omit fruit and almond extract.

EASY CRANBERRY PIE
Marjorie Carey, Belfry, Montana
(PICTURED ON PAGE 32)

2 cans (16 ounces *each*)
whole-berry cranberry sauce
1/4 cup packed brown sugar
2 tablespoons butter *or*
margarine, softened
Pastry for double-crust pie
(9 inches)

In a bowl, combine cranberry sauce, brown sugar and butter. Line pie plate with bottom pastry; add filling. Top with a lattice crust. Bake at 350° for 50-60 minutes or until the crust is lightly browned. **Yield:** 6-8 servings. **Editor's Note:** For a festively decorated pie, instead of making a lattice crust, use a cookie cutter to cut out Christmas tree shapes from the top pastry. Place the dough shapes on an ungreased baking sheet and bake at 350° for 10-15 minutes or until golden. Cool slightly; arrange on top of baked pie.

Quick & Easy

DAIRY STATE FUDGE
Jan Vande Slunt, Waupun, Wisconsin

1 package (8 ounces) cream
cheese, softened
2 tablespoons butter
(no substitutes)
2 pounds white almond bark,
broken into small pieces
1 to 1-1/2 cups chopped pecans,
walnuts *or* hickory nuts

In a mixing bowl, beat cream cheese until fluffy; set aside. In the top of a double boiler, melt butter. Add almond bark; heat and stir until melted and smooth. Pour over the cream cheese; beat until smooth and glossy, about 7-10 minutes. Stir in nuts. Pour into a greased 9-in. square pan. Store in the refrigerator. **Yield:** 64 pieces (about 1 inch).

PEANUTTY PIE
Dorothy Bowen, Thomasville, North Carolina
(PICTURED ON PAGE 25)

3/4 cup creamy peanut butter
1 box (16 ounces)
confectioners' sugar
1 package (8 ounces) cream
cheese, softened
1/3 cup light cream
1 carton (16 ounces) frozen
whipped topping, thawed,
divided
2 pastry shells (9 inches *each*),
baked

TOPPING:
1 cup (6 ounces) semisweet
chocolate chips
1/2 cup butter *or* margarine
3 tablespoons sugar
1/3 cup light cream
1 teaspoon vanilla extract
Chopped peanuts, optional

In a mixing bowl, beat peanut butter, confectioners' sugar, cream cheese and cream until smooth. Add a third of the whipped topping; blend thoroughly. Fold in the remaining whipped topping. Divide and spoon into pastry shells, mounding slightly at edges. Chill. For topping, heat chocolate chips, butter, sugar and cream in a small saucepan until chips are melted. Remove from the heat; add vanilla. Cover and let stand until cool. Spread over tops of pies to within 1 in. of crust. If desired, sprinkle with peanuts. Chill 4 hours before serving. Refrigerate any leftovers. **Yield:** 12-16 servings.

STRAWBERRY PRETZEL DESSERT
Aldene Belch, Flint, Michigan

2 cups crushed pretzels
(about 8 ounces)
3/4 cup butter *or* margarine,
melted
3 tablespoons sugar
FILLING:
2 cups whipped topping
1 package (8 ounces) cream
cheese, softened
1 cup sugar
TOPPING:
1 package (6 ounces)
strawberry-flavored gelatin
2 cups boiling water
2 packages (16 ounces *each*)
frozen sliced strawberries
with syrup, thawed
Additional whipped topping, optional

In a bowl, combine pretzels, butter and sugar. Press into the bottom of an ungreased 13-in. x 9-in. x 2-in. baking pan. Bake at 350° for 10 minutes. Cool. In a mixing bowl, beat whipped topping, cream cheese and sugar until smooth. Spread over pretzel crust. Chill. For topping, dissolve gelatin in boiling water in a large bowl. Stir in strawberries with syrup; chill until partially set. Carefully spoon over filling. Chill for 4-6 hours or until firm. Cut into squares; serve with a dollop of whipped topping if desired. **Yield:** 12-16 servings.

CRUSTS ALL WET? To avoid soggy crust in fruit pies, sprinkle bottom crust with sugar before adding fruit filling. For custard and pumpkin pies, prebake the crust for 5 minutes, then add the filling.

PIES are perfect because they offer plenty of versatility. Some are baked; some are refrigerated. Some satisfy everyday appetites; some turn special-occasion entertaining more special still. And all of them are scrumptious!

ENTICING SLICES. Clockwise from lower left: **Farm Apple Pan Pie**, **Very Raspberry Pie**, **Lemon Sour Cream Pie**, **Old-Fashioned Custard Pie**, **Pecan-Topped Pumpkin Pie**, **Cream Puff Pie**, **Rhubarb Meringue Pie** and **Peach Blueberry Pie** (all recipes on pages 76 and 77).

OLD-FASHIONED CUSTARD PIE
Maxine Linkenauger, Montverde, Florida
(PICTURED ON PAGE 75)

Pastry for single- or double-crust
  pie* (9 inches)
    4 eggs
2-1/2 cups milk
  1/2 cup sugar
    1 teaspoon vanilla extract
    1 teaspoon almond extract
    1 teaspoon salt
    1 teaspoon ground nutmeg

Line pie plate with bottom pastry; flute edges or prepare a braided crust (see Editor's Note). Bake at 400° for 10 minutes. Meanwhile, beat eggs in a large bowl. Add remaining ingredients; mix well. Pour into crust. Cover edges with foil. Bake for 20-25 minutes or until a knife inserted near the center comes out clean. Cool completely. Store in the refrigerator. *Editor's Note: Pastry for a double crust is needed only if a braided crust is desired. To prepare braided crust: Trim pastry even with the edge of the pie plate; brush with water. From the top pastry, cut 12 strips, each 1/4 in. thick. Using three strips at a time, braid pastry on edge of crust, attaching ends together. Press down gently. Bake as directed above. **Yield:** 6-8 servings.

RHUBARB MERINGUE PIE
Nancy Koopmann, Farley, Iowa
(PICTURED ON PAGE 74)

    3 tablespoons butter *or*
      margarine
    3 cups diced fresh *or* frozen
      rhubarb
    2 cups sugar, *divided*
    3 tablespoons cornstarch
  1/4 teaspoon salt
  1/2 cup light cream
    3 egg yolks, beaten
    1 pastry shell (9 inches), baked
MERINGUE:
    3 egg whites
  1/2 teaspoon vanilla extract
  1/4 teaspoon cream of tartar
    6 tablespoons sugar

In a saucepan, melt butter. Add rhubarb and 1-1/2 cups sugar; cook over medium heat until rhubarb is tender, about 10 minutes. Meanwhile, combine cornstarch, salt, cream and remaining sugar; beat well. Mix in egg yolks. Add a small amount of hot rhubarb mixture; mix well. Return all to pan; bring to a boil. Cook and stir for 2 minutes. Pour into pastry shell. For meringue, beat egg whites un-

til foamy; add vanilla and cream of tartar. Gradually add sugar, beating until stiff peaks form. Immediately spread over pie, sealing to the edge of the pastry. Bake at 350° for 12-15 minutes or until meringue is golden brown. Cool completely. Store in the refrigerator. **Yield:** 6-8 servings.

BANANA CREAM PIE
Nancy Eggleston, Prudenville, Michigan

    1 cup cold milk
    1 cup (8 ounces) sour cream
    1 package (3.4 ounces) instant
      vanilla pudding mix
    1 pastry shell (9 inches), baked
    3 medium firm bananas, sliced
      into 1/2-inch pieces
    1 carton (8 ounces) frozen
      whipped topping, thawed

In a mixing bowl, beat milk, sour cream and pudding mix until smooth. Place a third of the banana slices into pastry shell. Top with half of the pudding mixture. Repeat layers. Arrange the remaining bananas on top. Cover with whipped topping. Chill for at least 2 hours. **Yield:** 6-8 servings.

VERY RASPBERRY PIE
Kathy Jones, West Winfield, New York
(PICTURED ON PAGE 74)

RASPBERRY TOPPING:
    6 cups fresh raspberries,
      divided
    1 cup sugar
    3 tablespoons cornstarch
  1/2 cup water
CREAM FILLING:
    1 package (8 ounces) cream
      cheese, softened
    1 cup whipped topping
    1 cup confectioners' sugar
    1 graham cracker crust
      (9 inches)
Fresh mint, optional

Mash about 2 cups raspberries to measure 1 cup; place in a saucepan. Add sugar, cornstarch and water. Bring to a boil, stirring constantly; cook and stir 2 minutes longer. Strain to remove berry seeds if desired. Cool to room temperature, about 20 minutes. Meanwhile, for filling, beat cream cheese, whipped topping and confectioners' sugar in a mixing bowl. Spread in bottom of crust. Top with remaining raspberries. Pour cooled raspberry sauce over top. Refrigerate until set, about 3 hours. Store in the refrigerator. Garnish with mint if desired. **Yield:** 6-8 servings.

CREAM PUFF PIE
Holly Camozzi, Rohnert Park, California
(PICTURED ON PAGE 75)

CRUST:
  1/2 cup water
  1/4 cup butter *or* margarine
  1/2 teaspoon salt
  1/2 cup all-purpose flour
    2 eggs
FILLING:
  3/4 cup sugar
  1/3 cup all-purpose flour
  1/8 teaspoon salt
    2 eggs, lightly beaten
    2 cups milk
    1 teaspoon vanilla extract
    2 cups whipped cream, *divided*
Chocolate sauce *and/or* fresh
  raspberries, optional

In a large saucepan, bring water, butter and salt to a boil. Add flour all at once and stir until a smooth ball forms. Remove from the heat; beat in eggs, one at a time. Continue stirring vigorously until the mixture is smooth and shiny. Spread in the bottom and halfway up the sides of a well-greased 9-in. pie plate. Bake at 400° for 35-40 minutes. Cool completely. For filling, combine sugar, flour and salt in the top of a double boiler. Stir in eggs and milk until smooth. Cook over simmering water, stirring constantly, until mixture thickens. Remove from the heat; stir in vanilla. Cool. Fold in 1 cup of whipped cream. Pour into the crust. Top with remaining whipped cream. Chill for 2 hours. Garnish with chocolate sauce and/or raspberries if desired. **Yield:** 6-8 servings.

BLACKBERRY APPLE PIE
Fran Stanfield, Blanchester, Ohio

Pastry for a double-crust pie (9 inches)
    5 cups thinly sliced peeled
      baking apples (about
      4 medium)
    1 pint fresh blackberries, rinsed
      and drained
    1 tablespoon lemon juice
  3/4 cup sugar
    2 tablespoons cornstarch
    2 tablespoons butter *or*
      margarine
    1 egg, lightly beaten
    1 tablespoon water *or* milk
Additional sugar

Place bottom pastry in a 9-in. pie plate; top with a thin layer of apples. Combine blackberries and remaining apples in a large bowl; sprinkle with lemon juice. Add sugar and cornstarch and toss gent-

y. Spoon into pie shell; dot with butter. Top with a lattice crust; seal edges. Combine egg and water or milk; brush over lattice top and pie edges. Bake at 375° for 50 minutes or until filling is bubbly and apples are tender. Sprinkle with additional sugar. Serve warm or at room temperature. **Yield:** 6-8 servings.

LEMON SOUR CREAM PIE
Nancy Beran, St. Peter, Minnesota
(PICTURED ON PAGE 74)

     1 cup sugar
 1/4 cup cornstarch
 1/8 teaspoon salt
     1 cup milk
     3 egg yolks, beaten
 1/4 cup butter *or* margarine
 1/4 cup fresh lemon juice
     1 teaspoon grated lemon peel
     1 cup (8 ounces) sour cream
     1 pastry shell (9 inches), baked
MERINGUE:
     3 egg whites
 1/2 teaspoon vanilla extract
 1/4 teaspoon cream of tartar
     6 tablespoons sugar
Lemon peel strips, optional

In a saucepan, combine the sugar, cornstarch and salt. Gradually stir in the milk. Bring to a boil over medium heat, stirring constantly. Cook and stir for 2 minutes. Blend a small amount into egg yolks; mix well. Return all to pan; mix well. Cook and stir for 2 minutes. Remove from the heat. Add butter, lemon juice and peel; mix well. Set aside. For meringue, beat egg whites until foamy. Add vanilla and cream of tartar. Add sugar, 1 tablespoon at a time, beating until stiff peaks form; set aside. Fold sour cream into the lemon mixture; pour into pastry shell. Cover with meringue, sealing to edges of pastry. Bake at 350° for 12-15 minutes or until golden. Garnish with lemon peel strips if desired. Cool completely. Store in the refrigerator. **Yield:** 6-8 servings.

PEACH BLUEBERRY PIE
Sue Thumma, Shepherd, Michigan
(PICTURED ON PAGE 74)

     1 cup sugar
 1/3 cup all-purpose flour
 1/2 teaspoon ground cinnamon
 1/8 teaspoon ground allspice
     3 cups sliced peeled fresh peaches
     1 cup fresh blueberries
Pastry for double-crust pie (9 inches)
     1 tablespoon butter *or* margarine

Milk
Cinnamon-sugar

In a bowl, combine sugar, flour, cinnamon and allspice. Add the peaches and blueberries; toss gently. Line pie plate with bottom crust; add the filling. Dot with butter. Top with a lattice crust. Brush crust with milk; sprinkle with cinnamon-sugar. Bake at 400° for 40-45 minutes or until crust is golden brown and filling is bubbly. Cool completely. **Editor's Note:** Frozen fruit may be used if it is thawed and well drained. **Yield:** 6-8 servings.

FREEZER PEANUT BUTTER PIE
Nina Rufener, Mansfield, Ohio

     1 quart vanilla ice cream, softened, *divided*
     1 graham cracker crust (8 *or* 9 inches)
 1/2 cup peanut butter
 1/3 cup light corn syrup
Chocolate sauce
Chopped walnuts

Spread half of the ice cream into crust. Combine peanut butter and corn syrup; spread over ice cream. Spread evenly with remaining ice cream. Drizzle with chocolate sauce; top with nuts. Cover and freeze for 3-4 hours. Remove from freezer 15 minutes before serving. **Yield:** 6-8 servings. **Editor's Note:** If desired, recipe can be prepared several weeks before serving. Cover tightly with foil and freeze.

FARM APPLE PAN PIE
Dolores Skrout, Summerhill, Pennsylvania
(PICTURED ON PAGE 74)

EGG YOLK PASTRY:
     5 cups all-purpose flour
     4 teaspoons sugar
 1/2 teaspoon salt
 1/2 teaspoon baking powder
1-1/2 cups shortening
     2 egg yolks, lightly beaten
 3/4 cup cold water
FILLING:
     5 pounds tart apples, peeled and thinly sliced
     4 teaspoons lemon juice
 3/4 cup sugar
 3/4 cup packed brown sugar
     1 teaspoon ground cinnamon
 1/2 teaspoon ground nutmeg
 1/4 teaspoon salt
Milk
Additional sugar

In a bowl, combine flour, sugar, salt and baking powder; cut in shortening until the mixture resembles coarse crumbs. Combine yolks and cold water. Sprinkle over dry ingredients; toss with fork. If needed, add additional water, 1 tablespoon at a time, until the mixture can be formed into a ball. Divide dough in half. On a lightly floured surface, roll half of dough to fit a 15-in. x 10-in. x 1-in. baking pan. Sprinkle apples with lemon juice; arrange half of them over dough. Combine the sugars, cinnamon, nutmeg and salt; sprinkle half over apples. Top with remaining apples; sprinkle with remaining sugar mixture. Roll remaining pastry to fit pan; place on top of filling and seal edges. Brush with milk and sprinkle with sugar. Cut vents in top pastry. Bake at 400° for 50 minutes or until crust is golden brown and filling is bubbly. **Yield:** 18-24 servings.

PECAN-TOPPED PUMPKIN PIE
Jean Lockwood, Bayfield, Colorado
(PICTURED ON PAGE 75)

     2 eggs
 1/4 cup sugar
 1/4 cup packed brown sugar
     1 teaspoon all-purpose flour
     1 teaspoon pumpkin pie spice
 1/4 teaspoon salt
 2/3 cup cooked pumpkin
 2/3 cup milk
     1 unbaked deep-dish pastry shell (9 inches)
PECAN TOPPING:
     2 eggs
 1/2 cup dark corn syrup
     2 tablespoons brown sugar
     2 tablespoons molasses
     1 tablespoon all-purpose flour
     1 teaspoon vanilla extract
 1/2 teaspoon salt
 1/2 cup chopped pecans
     1 cup pecan halves

In a mixing bowl, beat eggs, sugars, flour, pie spice and salt until smooth. Mix in pumpkin. Gradually beat in milk. Pour into pastry shell. Bake at 425° for 10 minutes. Reduce the temperature to 350° and bake 15 minutes longer. For pecan topping, beat eggs in a mixing bowl until foamy. Add corn syrup, brown sugar, molasses, flour, vanilla and salt. Pour over filling. Sprinkle with chopped pecans; cover with pecan halves. Continue baking at 350° for 30-35 minutes or until set. Cool completely. Store in the refrigerator. **Yield:** 6-8 servings.

MARVELOUS MERINGUES. To cut meringue pie neatly, dip a sharp knife into water, shake off excess drops, cut a piece, then repeat the process.

SUNDAY SPECIALTIES. Pictured clockwise from top: Cornmeal Pie, Stove-Top Macaroni and Cheese, Salmon Cakes and Creamed Peas (all recipes on page 79).

My Most Memorable Meal

*In this chapter, six cooks share recipes for—
and memories of—their Mom's most treasured meal.*

FRUGAL MEAL IS FULL OF FLAVOR

"OUR usual daily menu was pretty basic," explains Imogene Hutton of Norton, Texas. "So it was quite a treat to be served these extra-special dishes for Sunday dinner.

"I still marvel at how Mama got this meal on the table so quickly after church," she recalls. "Of course, once we smelled the aroma of these foods, dinnertime couldn't come soon enough!

"This memorable meal always satisfied our hungry family fast—especially Dad. He'd start eating the salmon cakes as they were coming off the griddle.

"Canned salmon, peas, macaroni and cornmeal are economical foods to build a meal around," Imogene adds, "but we always regarded this meal as a treat."

Imogene has fond memories of the days when she gave her mother a hand in the kitchen. "Helping in the kitchen was a very special time for Mama and me. We even had fun doing dishes— she'd wash, I'd dry and we'd both sing!"

With these easy, economical recipes, Imogene proves you don't need to spend a fortune to serve a tasty meal. She's sure your family will sing its praises, too! Below, she shares recipes for her mom's most memorable meal.

CORNMEAL PIE

"MAMA always made two pies so we could have one for dessert on Monday. One pie served our family very nicely, and there was never any left over."

1 cup butter (no substitutes), softened
1-1/2 cups sugar
3 eggs
1-1/2 cups light corn syrup
1/2 cup milk
1 teaspoon vanilla extract
1/2 cup cornmeal
3 tablespoons all-purpose flour
2 unbaked pastry shells (9 inches)
Whipped cream, optional

In a large mixing bowl, cream the butter and sugar. Beat in eggs one at a time. Add corn syrup, milk and vanilla; mix well. Fold in cornmeal and flour. Pour into pastry shells. Bake at 350° for 25 minutes. Reduce heat to 300°; bake 20-25 minutes longer or until pies test done. Cool. Garnish with whipped cream if desired. **Yield:** 12-16 servings.

CREAMED PEAS

"OUR FOOD was pretty plain during the week, so I thought this white sauce made the peas 'extra fancy' and fitting for a Sunday meal."

1 tablespoon butter *or* margarine
1 tablespoon all-purpose flour
1/4 teaspoon salt
1/8 teaspoon pepper
1/2 cup milk
1 teaspoon sugar
1 package (10 ounces) frozen peas

In a medium saucepan, melt the butter. Add flour, salt and pepper; cook over low heat until bubbly. Gradually add milk and sugar; cook and stir until thickened. Cook peas according to package directions; drain. Stir into the sauce and heat through. **Yield:** 3-4 servings.

SALMON CAKES

"SALMON was a special treat on Sundays. We ate these cakes fast as Mama could fry them—she couldn't get them off the griddle fast enough."

2 eggs
1/4 cup heavy cream
1/4 cup cornmeal
2 tablespoons sliced green onions
2 tablespoons all-purpose flour
1/4 teaspoon baking powder
Pinch pepper
1/2 teaspoon salt, optional
1 can (14-3/4 ounces) salmon, drained, skinned and boned
1 to 2 tablespoons butter *or* margarine

In a medium bowl, beat the eggs. Add cream, cornmeal, green onions, flour, baking powder, pepper and salt if desired. Flake salmon into bowl; blend gently. Melt butter in a skillet or griddle; drop salmon mixture by 1/3 cupfuls and fry over medium heat for 5 minutes per side or until lightly browned. Serve hot. **Yield:** 3-4 servings (six patties).

STOVE-TOP MACARONI AND CHEESE

"WHEN the cheese melted, it covered all the macaroni. I loved to dig in and see how many strings of cheese would follow my spoonful."

1 box (7 ounces) elbow macaroni
1/4 cup butter *or* margarine
1/4 cup all-purpose flour
1/2 teaspoon salt
Pinch pepper
2 cups milk
2 cups (8 ounces) shredded cheddar cheese
Paprika, optional

Cook macaroni according to package directions. Meanwhile, in a medium saucepan, melt butter over medium heat. Stir in flour, salt and pepper; cook until bubbly. Gradually add milk; cook and stir until thickened. Stir in cheese until melted. Drain macaroni; add to cheese sauce and stir to coat. Sprinkle with paprika if desired. **Yield:** 4-6 servings.

SPECIAL-REQUEST RECIPES. Pictured clockwise from top: Bananas 'n' Cream Bundt Cake, Sweet-and-Sour Green Beans, Pork Roast with Spiced Apples and Spoon Rolls (all recipes on page 81).

PORK ROAST WAS SUNDAY'S BEST

"THIS IS the meal I always picked when it was my turn to choose what our family would have for Sunday dinner," recalls Oma Rollison of El Cajon, California.

"Mother's pork roast was so good and tender, and her spiced apples were the next best thing to candy!"

Some of Oma's most cherished childhood memories are of helping her mother prepare this special meal. "Mother let me spoon the dough for the rolls into the pan, and that made me feel so important," she reflects.

Oma's father, meanwhile, thought the highlight of the meal was dessert. When his wife's delicious cake was served, he would say, "It makes my taste buds stand up and applaud!"

"I can still hear him saying that," Oma smiles, "and that memory of my father still comes to mind whenever I make Mother's favorite Bananas 'n' Cream Bundt Cake."

When Oma prepares these delightful dishes, she remembers all the wonderful memories she and her mother cooked up in the kitchen.

Your family will applaud every course of this meal. So try it some Sunday soon...or on any other day. Below, Oma shares all recipes for her mom's most memorable meal.

SPOON ROLLS

"THE BATTER for these rolls may be stored in the refrigerator for up to 4 days, so this is a great way to treat your family to homemade rolls without the extra preparation each time. My mother raised eight children, and we had these delicious 'from-scratch' rolls often."

- **1 package (1/4 ounce) active dry yeast**
- **2 cups warm water (110° to 115°)**
- **1/2 cup butter or margarine, melted**
- **1 egg, beaten**
- **1/4 cup sugar**
- **4 cups self-rising flour**

In a large mixing bowl, dissolve yeast in warm water. Let stand for 5 minutes. Add butter, egg and sugar; mix well. Stir in flour until thoroughly combined (batter will be soft). Cover and refrigerate overnight. Spoon batter into greased or paper-lined muffin cups. Bake at 375° for 25-30 minutes or until golden brown. **Yield:** 16 rolls. **If Cooking for Two:** Freeze baked rolls in freezer bags; thaw and reheat as needed.

Quick & Easy

SWEET-AND-SOUR GREEN BEANS

"GREEN BEANS are the perfect accompaniment to Mother's pork roast. The flavors are compatible and blend well. I've never cooked any other vegetable dish when I make this pork roast."

- **4 bacon strips**
- **1/2 cup chopped onion**
- **2 tablespoons all-purpose flour**
- **3/4 cup water**
- **1/3 cup cider vinegar**
- **2 tablespoons sugar**
- **6 to 8 cups green beans, cooked and drained**

In a skillet, cook bacon until crisp; drain, reserving 2 tablespoons of drippings. Crumble the bacon and set aside. Saute the onion in drippings until tender. Stir in flour until thoroughly combined. Add water, vinegar and sugar. Cook and stir until thickened and bubbly; cook and stir 2 minutes more. Gently stir in beans and heat through. Sprinkle with bacon. Serve immediately. **Yield:** 8-10 servings.

PORK ROAST WITH SPICED APPLES

"THE FINE FLAVOR of this pork roast is further enhanced when spicy-sweet apples are spooned over slices of the meat. This wonderful recipe made pork my favorite of all meats."

- **1 teaspoon salt**
- **1 teaspoon ground ginger**
- **1/2 teaspoon ground nutmeg**
- **1/2 teaspoon ground cinnamon**
- **1 boneless rolled pork loin roast (4 to 5 pounds)**

SPICED APPLES:
- **1/4 cup honey**
- **1/2 cup water**
- **1 tablespoon lemon juice**
- **1/4 teaspoon ground ginger**
- **1/4 teaspoon ground nutmeg**
- **1/4 teaspoon ground cinnamon**
- **2 medium apples, peeled, cored and sliced**

Combine salt, ginger, nutmeg and cinnamon; rub over roast. Place roast, fat side up, on a rack in a shallow roasting pan. Insert a meat thermometer. Bake, uncovered, at 325° for 2 to 2-1/2 hours or until thermometer registers 160°. Cover and let stand 15 minutes before slicing. In a medium skillet, combine the first six spiced apples ingredients; bring to a boil. Reduce heat and simmer, uncovered, until slightly thickened. Add apples; simmer, uncovered, until apples are just tender, stirring gently. Serve with sliced pork roast. **Yield:** 8-10 servings. **If Cooking for Two:** Both the pork roast and apples will freeze well (separately). Store individual portions in airtight containers.

BANANAS 'N' CREAM BUNDT CAKE

"THIS absolutely scrumptious cake needs no icing...just a dusting of confectioners' sugar. Even though this recipe has been a 'family secret' for years, I'm delighted to share it with you."

- **1/3 cup shortening**
- **1-1/4 cups sugar**
- **2 eggs**
- **1 teaspoon vanilla extract**
- **1-1/4 cups mashed ripe bananas (about 3 medium)**
- **2 cups all-purpose flour**
- **1-1/4 teaspoons baking powder**
- **1 teaspoon baking soda**
- **1/2 teaspoon salt**
- **1 cup (8 ounces) sour cream**
- **3/4 cup chopped walnuts**
Confectioners' sugar

In a mixing bowl, cream the shortening and sugar. Add the eggs, one at a time, beating well after each addition. Blend in vanilla. Add bananas and mix well. Combine flour, baking powder, baking soda and salt; add to the creamed mixture alternately with sour cream, stirring just until combined. Stir in walnuts. Pour into a greased and floured 10-in. fluted tube pan. Bake at 350° for 50 minutes or until cake tests done. Cool 10 minutes in pan before removing to a wire rack to cool completely. Dust with confectioners' sugar before serving. **Yield:** 12-16 servings.

HOLIDAY FARE. Pictured clockwise from top left: Apricot Salad, Turkey with Corn-Bread Dressing, Harvest Sweet Potato Pie and Creamy Broccoli Casserole (all recipes on page 83).

COUNTRY COOKING'S ALL IN THE FAMILY

"MY MOTHER came from a family of great country cooks and was known for her Southern hospitality," recalls Fae Fisher of Callao, Virginia. "Family and friends were invited for meals throughout the whole year.

"One of my most cherished memories is gathering around the dining room table and my father saying grace to thank God for all of our many blessings—including this special holiday meal," adds Fae. "Mother last prepared this meal in 1940, and it included all our family favorites."

Fae knows you'll agree that these wonderfully traditional Southern dishes would make great family fare anywhere in the country. One taste and you'll see that her mother did come from a family of good cooks. Below, Fae shares recipes for her mom's most memorable meal.

HARVEST SWEET POTATO PIE

"THE PIES were baked a few days before the holiday gathering and then placed in a tall pie safe on our back porch. My father called this 'royal pie', fit for a king with its deliciously different flavor. This is another hand-me-down recipe, a treasure in our family."

        4 eggs
        1 can (12 ounces) evaporated
          milk
    1-1/4 cups sugar
        3/4 cup butter *or* margarine,
          melted
        2 teaspoons ground cinnamon
        2 teaspoons pumpkin pie spice
        1 teaspoon vanilla extract
        1 teaspoon lemon extract
        1/2 teaspoon ground nutmeg
        1/2 teaspoon salt
        4 cups mashed cooked sweet
          potatoes
        2 unbaked pastry shells
          (9 inches)
    Whipped cream, optional

In a mixing bowl, combine first 10 ingredients; mix well. Beat in sweet potatoes. Pour into pie shells. Bake at 425° for 15 minutes. Reduce heat to 350°; bake 30-35 minutes longer or until a knife inserted near the center comes out clean. Cool completely. Serve with whipped cream if desired. Store in the refrigerator. **Yield:** 12-16 servings.

CREAMY BROCCOLI CASSEROLE

"MOTHER called this her secret recipe, and to this day, I'm not quite sure I have all the ingredients she used in it. But it still tastes great, so who knows—maybe I acquired some of her 'touch'. After I was married, this casserole became my husband's favorite vegetable dish."

        2 eggs
        1 can (10-3/4 ounces)
          condensed cream of
          mushroom soup, undiluted
        1 cup mayonnaise
        3/4 cup chopped pecans
        1 medium onion, chopped
        2 packages (10 ounces *each*)
          frozen chopped broccoli,
          cooked and drained
        1 cup (4 ounces) shredded
          cheddar cheese
        1 tablespoon butter *or*
          margarine, melted
        1/4 cup soft bread crumbs

In a bowl, beat eggs; add soup, mayonnaise, pecans and onion. Stir in broccoli; pour into a greased 2-qt. shallow baking dish. Sprinkle with the cheese. Combine butter and bread crumbs; sprinkle on top. Bake, uncovered, at 350° for 30 minutes. **Yield:** 8-10 servings.

TURKEY WITH CORN-BREAD DRESSING

"THE DRESSING was always my favorite part of the meal. I can still smell the wonderful aroma that filled the house while the turkey roasted in our wood stove. We could hardly wait to sit down and eat!"

    CORN BREAD:
        3 cups self-rising cornmeal
        1 cup self-rising flour
    1-1/4 cups chopped celery
        1/3 cup chopped onion
        1/2 teaspoon celery seed
        2 cups milk
        1/4 cup shortening, melted
        1 egg
    DRESSING:
        1/2 cup chopped fresh parsley
        1 to 2 tablespoons poultry
          seasoning
        3/4 teaspoon pepper
        3 eggs, beaten
        1 cup butter *or* margarine,
          melted, *divided*
        1 turkey (10 to 12 pounds)

Combine the first five ingredients in a large bowl. Combine milk, shortening and egg; pour over cornmeal mixture and mix well. Pour into a greased 13-in. x 9-in. x 2-in. baking pan. Bake at 350° for 50 minutes or until bread tests done. Cool. Crumble corn bread into a large bowl. Add parsley, poultry seasoning and pepper; toss. Combine eggs and 3/4 cup butter; add to the corn bread mixture, stirring gently to mix. Just before baking, stuff the turkey with dressing. Skewer or fasten openings. Tie drumsticks together. Place on a rack in a roasting pan. Brush with remaining butter. Place remaining dressing in a greased baking dish; cover and refrigerate until ready to bake. Bake turkey at 325° for 4-1/2 to 5 hours or until thermometer reads 180°. When turkey begins to brown, cover lightly with a tent of aluminum foil. Bake extra dressing at 325° for 1 hour. When turkey is done, allow to stand for 20 minutes before carving. Remove all dressing to a serving bowl. **Yield:** 8-10 servings (10 cups dressing).

APRICOT SALAD

"COLORFUL gelatin salad adds a spot of brightness to any table. It blends well with this holiday feast. We children didn't know if it should be a salad or dessert, with its smooth texture and delicate flavor."

        2 packages (3 ounces *each*)
          apricot-flavored gelatin
        2 cups boiling water
        1 package (8 ounces) cream
          cheese, softened
        1 cup milk
        1 can (20 ounces) crushed
          pineapple, undrained
        1 carton (4 ounces) frozen
          whipped topping, thawed

Dissolve gelatin in boiling water and set aside. In a mixing bowl, beat cream cheese until smooth. Gradually beat in milk until smooth. Stir in gelatin. Add pineapple and mix well. Chill. When mixture begins to thicken, fold in whipped topping. Pour into a 2-1/2-qt. serving bowl. Chill for at least 2 hours. **Yield:** 8-10 servings.

CHERISHED CHURCH DISHES. Pictured clockwise from top left: Refrigerator Bran Muffins, Deviled Baked Steak, Frozen Fruit Salad and Creamed Green Beans (all recipes on page 85).

BIRTHDAY DINNER WAS ALWAYS A DELIGHT

'MOST folks know that a church supper is the best place to enjoy a delicious variety of foods," says Betty Shaw of Weirton, West Virginia. "I learned this very young because I was a 'preacher's kid'.

"As we moved from parish to parish, Mother collected favorite recipes from church members," Betty fondly recalls. "She recorded these in a special cookbook, along with the person's name.

"On our birthdays, we kids had the privilege of leafing through this treasured cookbook to choose what we wanted to eat. As we enjoyed the meal Mother prepared, we'd smile, laugh and maybe even shed a tear as we remembered the parishioners who'd contributed those recipes."

This combination of cherished recipes is one of Betty's most memorable meals. Whenever she pulls out this collection of menu items, Betty recalls some treasured times seasoned with tasty memories. Below, she shares recipes for her mom's most memorable meal.

DEVILED BAKED STEAK

"WHEN WE were growing up, this was one of my brother's favorite dishes. We girls often thought Mother made this just for him, but she knew we enjoyed it, too! Since I'm the oldest, my brothers and sisters often 'come home' to my house, and I make baked steak for them."

- 2 pounds boneless round steak (1 inch thick)
- 3/4 cup all-purpose flour
- 1 teaspoon dry mustard
- 1 teaspoon salt
- 1/2 teaspoon pepper
- 2 to 3 tablespoons cooking oil
- 1 medium onion, sliced
- 1 can (14-1/2 ounces) tomatoes with liquid, cut up
- 1 carrot, diced
- 1 teaspoon brown sugar
- 2 teaspoons Worcestershire sauce
- Cooked noodles or mashed potatoes

Trim excess fat from steak; cut into serving-size pieces. Combine flour, mustard, salt and pepper; pound into steak. In a skillet, brown steak, half at a time, in oil. Place meat in a large baking dish; top with onion. Combine tomatoes, carrot, brown sugar and Worcestershire sauce; pour over meat. Cover and bake at 325° for 1-1/2 to 2 hours or until meat is tender. Remove meat to a serving platter. If desired, simmer tomato-onion mixture until it is reduced to a thick gravy. Serve meat and gravy over noodles or mashed potatoes. **Yield:** 6-8 servings.

> **MUFFIN MAGIC.** When muffins get done ahead of serving time and you want to keep them warm, loosen them from their cups, tilt slightly and put back in the oven. The muffins won't steam on the bottom.

 Quick & Easy

REFRIGERATOR BRAN MUFFINS

"WHEN I TOLD THEM I was submitting some church-supper recipes, everyone in the family said I should be sure to send along this one."

- 4 eggs
- 1 quart buttermilk
- 1 cup vegetable oil
- 1 cup sugar
- 6 cups (10 ounces) bran flakes with raisins
- 1/2 to 1 cup raisins
- 5 cups all-purpose flour
- 5 teaspoons baking soda
- 1 teaspoon salt

In a large mixing bowl, beat eggs, buttermilk, oil and sugar. Stir in cereal and raisins. Sift together flour, baking soda and salt; add to egg mixture. Stir just until all ingredients are moistened. If desired, store batter, covered, in the refrigerator for up to 7 days. To bake, gently stir batter; fill greased muffin cups two-thirds full. Bake at 400° for 15-20 minutes or until golden brown. Serve warm. (All of the batter does not need to be baked at once.) **Yield:** about 3 dozen. **If Cooking for Two:** Bake muffins and freeze to enjoy months later.

FROZEN FRUIT SALAD

"THIS delicious recipe works well as a salad or dessert—my family always said they liked it better than ice cream! I prepare it often because it's so convenient to have in the freezer. It can be made well in advance of the time you plan to serve it."

- 1 can (14 ounces) sweetened condensed milk
- 1 can (21 ounces) peach or cherry pie filling
- 1 can (15 ounces) mandarin oranges, drained
- 1 can (20 ounces) crushed pineapple, drained
- 2/3 cup chopped pecans or walnuts
- 1 carton (8 ounces) frozen whipped topping, thawed
- Lettuce leaves, optional

In a large bowl, combine milk and pie filling. Add oranges, pineapple and nuts. Gently fold in whipped topping. Spread in a 13-in. x 9-in. x 2-in. pan. Cover and freeze. Remove from the freezer 15 minutes before serving. Cut into squares; serve on lettuce-lined plates if desired. **Yield:** 12-15 servings.

CREAMED GREEN BEANS

"A FAMILY FAVORITE for years, this recipe is one I make often because it can easily be doubled and prepared ahead. It's a must on the menu when my nephews come for dinner!"

- 3 tablespoons butter or margarine, *divided*
- 1/2 cup cornflakes, crumbled
- 1 tablespoon all-purpose flour
- 1/4 teaspoon salt
- 1/4 teaspoon pepper
- 1 teaspoon instant minced onion
- 1 teaspoon sugar
- 1 cup (8 ounces) sour cream
- 4 to 6 cups French-style green beans, cooked and drained
- 1 cup (4 ounces) shredded sharp cheddar or Swiss cheese

In a small saucepan, melt 1 tablespoon butter; stir in cornflakes and set aside. Melt remaining butter in a large saucepan. Stir in flour, salt, pepper, onion and sugar; heat and stir until bubbly. Reduce heat; add the sour cream and stir until smooth. Cook and stir over low heat for 2 minutes (do not boil). Fold in the beans. Spread into a greased 1-1/2-qt. baking dish. Sprinkle cheese evenly over the top. Sprinkle with cornflake mixture. Bake, uncovered, at 400° for 20 minutes or until heated through. **Yield:** 6-8 servings.

"MY FATHER'S family has roots in Trier, Germany," says Barbara White of Cross Plains, Wisconsin. "So it's not surprising that my most memorable meal features this delicious, hearty sauerbraten.

"Each year, Dad, Mom and we kids would help prepare this special meal for our New Year's Day open house. Friends began looking forward to this meal so much that I'm sure they would have complained if my parents changed the menu!"

In fact, Barb adds, her parents' New Year's Day meal became so well-known that they were invited to demonstrate how to cook it on a local television show!

Barbara guarantees that once you sample these traditional German dishes, they'll fast become family favorites. Below, she shares recipes for her mom's—and dad's—most memorable meal.

POTATO DUMPLINGS

"WHEN I was a child, I loved to watch the cooking dumplings pop to the top of the pot of boiling water. We youngsters always had two helpings...one with sauerbraten gravy and the other with warm plum jam on top!"

CROUTONS:
- 1/4 cup butter *or* margarine
- 3 slices dry bread, cut into small cubes

DUMPLINGS:
- 4 medium potatoes, peeled and quartered
- 1 cup all-purpose flour
- 1 teaspoon baking powder
- 1 teaspoon salt
- 2 teaspoons ground nutmeg
- 2 eggs, lightly beaten
- 2 teaspoons butter *or* margarine
- 2 tablespoons dry bread crumbs

For croutons, melt butter in a small skillet; brown bread cubes. Set aside. In a saucepan, boil potatoes in water to cover until tender. Cool; rice potatoes and place in a large bowl. Add flour, baking powder, salt and nutmeg. Stir in eggs; beat until mixture holds its shape. With lightly floured hands, shape about 2 tablespoons dough into a ball, placing a few croutons in center of each ball. Repeat with remaining dough and croutons. Refrigerate for 1 hour. Drop dumplings into boiling salted water (2 teaspoons salt to 1 quart water). Simmer, uncovered, for 10 minutes. Drain. Melt butter in a small skillet; cook and stir the bread crumbs until lightly browned. Sprinkle over dumplings. **Yield:** 15 dumplings.

SWEET-AND-SOUR RED CABBAGE

"THE TOUCH of tartness in this cabbage is wonderful with the sauerbraten. This is one part of the meal that is even tastier if it can be made ahead."

- 2 tablespoons bacon drippings *or* cooking oil
- 1/4 cup packed brown sugar
- 3 tablespoons vinegar
- 1 cup water
- 1/4 teaspoon salt
- Dash pepper
- 4 cups shredded red cabbage
- 2 apples, peeled and sliced

In a large skillet, combine drippings or oil, brown sugar, vinegar, water, salt and pepper. Cook for 2-3 minutes or until hot, stirring occasionally. Add cabbage; cover and cook for 10 minutes over medium-low heat, stirring occasionally. Add apples; cook, uncovered, for about 10 minutes more or until tender, stirring occasionally. **Yield:** 6-8 servings. **If Cooking for Two:** Cabbage keeps well when frozen in airtight containers.

SAUERBRATEN

"THE WHOLE FAMILY helped prepare this sauerbraten. We children had fun mixing and pounding the spices, then Dad rubbed them into the meat. The tantalizing aromas escalated as the sauerbraten cooked."

- 1 tablespoon whole peppercorns
- 1 tablespoon whole allspice
- 1 tablespoon salt
- 1 beef rump roast (4 to 5 pounds)
- 4 bacon strips, diced
- 1 cup vinegar
- 1 cup water
- 12 whole peppercorns
- 12 whole allspice
- 1 large onion, sliced
- 2 bay leaves
- 1 jar (12 ounces) plum preserves
- 2 gingersnaps, crushed
- 1 cup beef broth *or* port wine
- 1/2 cup all-purpose flour

Place the tablespoon of peppercorns and allspice in a cloth bag; pound to a powder with a hammer. Mix in salt; rub over roast. Set aside. In a large Dutch oven, cook bacon for 3-4 minutes or until fat begins to cook out. Push bacon to edge of pan. Add roast; brown on all sides. Add vinegar, water, whole peppercorns and allspice, onion and bay leaves; bring to a boil. Reduce heat; cover and simmer for 2 hours. Stir in preserves and gingersnaps; cook 1 hour longer or until meat is tender. Chill roast overnight in cooking liquid. The next day, skim off fat. Heat roast slowly in cooking liquid until heated through, about 1 hour. Remove roast and keep warm. Strain cooking liquid; return 3-1/2 cups to pan. Combine broth or wine and flour; stir into cooking liquid. Cook and stir until thickened and bubbly; cook and stir 1 minute more. Slice roast and serve with gravy. **Yield:** 12-14 servings. **If Cooking for Two:** Freeze serving-size portions of meat and gravy together in airtight containers.

PEACH KUCHEN

"KUCHEN IS a fitting dessert for this German meal. It's not too sweet, and you can use virtually any of your favorite fruits. A dollop of whipped cream on top of this warm and fresh dessert was an added treat!"

CRUST:
- 1 cup all-purpose flour
- 1/4 cup confectioners' sugar
- 1/4 teaspoon salt
- 1/2 cup butter *or* margarine

FILLING:
- 2 cans (one 29 ounces, one 16 ounces) sliced peaches, drained
- 2 eggs
- 1 cup sugar
- 1/4 teaspoon salt
- 3 tablespoons all-purpose flour
- 1 cup (8 ounces) sour cream

In a bowl, combine flour, confectioners' sugar and salt. Cut in butter to form a dough. Pat lightly into an ungreased 11-in. x 7-in. x 2-in. baking pan. Arrange peaches over the crust; set aside. In another bowl, beat eggs. Whisk in sugar, salt, flour and sour cream until mixture is smooth. Pour over the peaches. Bake at 450° for 10 minutes. Reduce heat to 325°; bake 35 minutes more or until center is set. Serve warm or chilled. Store in the refrigerator. **Yield:** 8-10 servings.

CLASSIC CHICKEN. Pictured clockwise from top: World's Best Lemon Pie, Marinated Tomatoes, Farmhouse Chicken and Biscuits and Cucumbers in Cream (all recipes on page 89).

LABOR OF LOVE LIVES ON

"SUNDAY was the only time Mother could make our favorite chicken dinner because it took all day long to prepare," recalls Phyllis Kirsling of Junction City, Wisconsin.

"First, she'd select a nice chicken from the farmyard, then she got to work cooking the chicken and biscuits over a wood fire in her cookstove. After simmering all day, the chicken was always moist and delicious.

"We children would help Mother by going to the garden and gathering fresh produce for the accompanying salads—Marinated Tomatoes and Cucumbers in Cream. To top off this marvelous meal, we'd each be served a generous slice of refreshing lemon meringue pie.

"Making our family's favorite meal was a labor of love for Mother and it became a treasured tradition for us," she remembers.

Today Phyllis carries on the tradition by preparing this special meal for her own family frequently. "Happily, with all my modern conveniences, I don't need a whole day to get it ready!" she notes. Below, Phyllis shares recipes for her mom's most memorable meal.

FARMHOUSE CHICKEN AND BISCUITS

"MOTHER had two special ways of fixing chicken—browning serving-size pieces in fresh butter, or preparing this delicious sauce with the chicken added. Either way, our family loved Mother's chicken!"

- 1 broiler-fryer chicken (3-1/2 to 4 pounds), cut up
- 2 carrots, sliced
- 2 celery ribs with leaves, sliced
- 1 green onion, sliced
- 5 peppercorns
- 1 teaspoon salt
- 6 cups water
- 6 tablespoons butter *or* margarine
- 1/2 cup all-purpose flour
- 1/4 teaspoon pepper
- Homemade *or* purchased biscuits, warmed

Combine the first seven ingredients in a Dutch oven; cover and simmer until the chicken is tender, about 45 minutes. Remove vegetables and chicken from broth; set vegetables aside, and skin, bone and cube the chicken. Strain and reserve 3 cups of the broth. In a large saucepan, melt butter; add flour and pepper. Cook and stir over medium heat until bubbly. Gradually stir in the reserved broth; bring to a boil, stirring constantly. Boil for 1 minute. Add chicken and vegetables; heat through. Serve over biscuits. **Yield:** 6-8 servings.

CUCUMBERS IN CREAM

"WE HAD an enormous vegetable garden, so we enjoyed freshly picked cucumbers in summer. After the cucumbers were sliced and soaked awhile in salt water, Mother added thick cream, which she carefully scooped from the top of some fresh milk."

- 3 medium cucumbers, peeled and thinly sliced
- 1 medium onion, sliced
- 2 cups water
- 1/2 teaspoon salt
- 3/4 cup heavy cream
- 1/4 cup sugar
- 1/4 cup vinegar
- Chopped fresh parsley, optional

In a bowl, combine cucumbers, onion, water and salt. Let stand for 1 hour; drain and rinse. In a serving bowl, mix cream, sugar and vinegar. Add cucumbers and onion; toss gently. Sprinkle with parsley if desired. **Yield:** 6-8 servings.

MARINATED TOMATOES

"OUR GARDEN always yielded a large crop of tomatoes, but we never complained. In season, we ate tomatoes every day—and this salad was one of our favorites. Mother also grew her own herbs...dill, basil and thyme.

The fresh flavor of basil enhances the great taste of summer tomatoes."

- 4 medium tomatoes, sliced
- 3 tablespoons vegetable oil
- 2 tablespoons minced fresh basil *or* 2 teaspoons dried basil
- 1 tablespoon vinegar
- 1 teaspoon sugar

Place the tomatoes in a shallow serving dish. In a bowl, mix oil, basil, vinegar and sugar. Pour over tomatoes. Cover and refrigerate for several hours. **Yield:** 6-8 servings.

> **STOP SHELL SHRINKAGE!** To prevent your pie shell from shrinking as it bakes, put rolled pastry in a pie plate, then place an empty pie plate inside it. Bake 10 minutes. Remove the empty plate; continue baking until crust is brown.

WORLD'S BEST LEMON PIE

"MOTHER'S PIES were always so wonderful, with tender, flaky crusts. Through the year we enjoyed berry and apple pies, but in summer the order of the day was lemon meringue—so light and refreshing!"

- 1 cup sugar
- 1/4 cup cornstarch
- 3 tablespoons all-purpose flour
- 1/4 teaspoon salt
- 2 cups water
- 3 egg yolks, beaten
- 1 tablespoon butter *or* margarine
- 1/4 cup lemon juice
- 1 teaspoon grated lemon peel
- 1 pastry shell (9 inches), baked

MERINGUE:
- 3 egg whites
- 1/4 teaspoon salt
- 1/2 cup sugar

In a medium saucepan, combine sugar, cornstarch, flour and salt. Gradually stir in water. Cook and stir over medium heat until thickened and bubbly. Reduce heat; cook and stir 2 minutes more. Remove from the heat. Gradually stir 1 cup into egg yolks; return all to saucepan. Bring to a boil. Cook and stir for 2 minutes. Remove from the heat. Stir in the butter, lemon juice and peel until smooth. Pour into pastry shell. In a mixing bowl, beat egg whites and salt until stiff but not dry peaks form. Gradually beat in sugar until soft peaks form. Spread over pie, sealing edges to pastry. Bake at 350° for 12-15 minutes or until meringue is golden. Cool. Store any leftovers in the refrigerator. **Yield:** 6-8 servings.

Meals in Minutes

Six cooks across the country provide complete quick meals that take you from start to serving in just half an hour!

Tonight, Make It Italian!

WHEN Kelly Azzopardi of Harrow, Ontario finishes up her daily duties as a school bus driver—a job that keeps her on the road 40 miles every weekday—she doesn't have much time for relaxation.

"My husband's a hardworking plastic mold-maker who comes home hungry, and we have a 5-year-old daughter," she informs. "Plus, in my 'spare' time, I make crafts for a local shop. So, while cooking is also among my favorite hobbies, I usually can't afford to spend too much time in the kitchen."

That's where this complete meal comes in. "It's on our menu, in one form or another, just about every week," Kelly reports.

Her speedy supper starts with an exhilarating new approach to everyday poultry—Zesty Mozzarella Chicken.

"My husband *loves* cheese," she notes, "and it makes my coating moister than most. Using boneless chicken, meanwhile, cuts the cooking time.

"The Cucumber-Dill Pasta Salad is an especially quick creation—I came up with it when I was asked to bring a dish to a last-minute get-together!

"My Easy Cherry Tarts were actually my grandmother's specialty. We all thought she spent *hours* making them. Was I surprised when she showed me her secret of using canned pie filling and premade crusts."

Go ahead and surprise your family. With this yummy meal, they'll love having a "fast one" pulled on them!

ZESTY MOZZARELLA CHICKEN

- 1 egg white, lightly beaten
- 2 tablespoons milk
- 1 cup dry bread crumbs
- 2 tablespoons grated Parmesan cheese
- 1/4 teaspoon *each* salt, pepper, garlic powder, cayenne pepper and dried oregano
- 8 boneless skinless chicken breast halves
- 1/4 cup butter *or* margarine
- 1 can (8 ounces) tomato sauce
- 1 teaspoon dried basil
- 1 cup (4 ounces) shredded mozzarella cheese

In a shallow bowl, combine egg white and milk. In another bowl, combine the bread crumbs, Parmesan cheese and seasonings. Dip each chicken breast in the egg white mixture, then in the crumb mixture. Melt butter in a skillet; brown chicken on both sides until no longer pink and juices run clear. Meanwhile, heat tomato sauce and basil until warm. When chicken is done, sprinkle with mozzarella cheese. Remove from the heat and cover for 2-3 minutes or until cheese melts. Serve with tomato-basil sauce. **Yield:** 4 servings.

CUCUMBER-DILL PASTA SALAD

- 3 cups cooked pasta
- 1/2 cup thinly sliced carrot
- 1/2 cup thinly sliced celery
- 1 cup parboiled broccoli florets
- 1 green onion, thinly sliced
- 1/4 cup chopped onion
- 1/2 to 3/4 cup bottled cucumber salad dressing
- 1 teaspoon dill weed

Salt and pepper to taste

Combine all ingredients in a large salad bowl. Chill until serving time. **Yield:** 4-6 servings.

EASY CHERRY TARTS

- 1 can (21 ounces) cherry pie filling
- 1 package (4 ounces) single-serve graham cracker crusts (6 crusts)

Frozen whipped topping, thawed
Chocolate sprinkles

Divide pie filling among the crusts. Top with whipped topping and chocolate sprinkles. Chill. **Yield:** 6 servings.

Fool-Proof Family Favorite

IF time's suddenly grown tight and her hungry husband is due home any minute, Karen Grimes of Stephens City, Virginia knows just what to do: start preparing one of his favorite meals!

"When I came across the recipe for Cheeseburger Skillet Dinner," Karen says of the main course for the ready-in-30-minutes-or-less menu she shares here, "I knew immediately Tim would love it, since he's a cheeseburger fan.

"And did he ever! The first time I made it, he told me I could fix it *every* week if I wanted to."

With a very active toddler son, Karen reports that she does turn to this "Meal in Minutes" frequently. "It's speedy," she notes. "And the ingredients are almost always on hand.

"Actually, the skillet dinner is doubly quick. The leftovers—if there are any!—can be reheated to make a second meal as tasty as the first.

"Quick Italian Salad is a basic one I tossed together. It's a nice light way to work extra vegetables into the meal.

"For my Fruit Fool dessert, most often I'll use apricot filling…apricot was one of my favorite fruits when I was growing up, and both my 'guys' like it in this recipe besides. But peach works as well. On occasion, I've been known to substitute apple or cherry pie filling, too."

The "makings" you need for Karen's flavorful menu probably are already in your kitchen…and time's no problem no matter how little there is!

QUICK ITALIAN SALAD

Salad greens
Sliced tomatoes, zucchini,
  mushrooms and green
  pepper *or* vegetables of your
  choice
  1 cup vegetable oil
1/2 cup white wine vinegar
  1 garlic clove, minced
  2 tablespoons minced fresh
    parsley
  1 tablespoon grated Parmesan
    cheese
1-1/2 teaspoons dried basil
  1 teaspoon dried oregano
1/2 teaspoon pepper

Arrange greens and vegetables in a salad bowl or on individual salad plates. In a jar with a tight-fitting lid, combine all remaining ingredients; shake well. Serve over salad. **Yield:** 1-1/2 cups dressing.

CHEESEBURGER SKILLET DINNER

  1 package (7-1/4 ounces)
    macaroni and cheese
  1 pound ground turkey *or* beef
1/2 cup chopped onion
  1 package (16 ounces) frozen
    mixed vegetables
1/3 cup ketchup
1/4 cup water
1/2 teaspoon prepared mustard
1/4 teaspoon garlic powder
3/4 cup shredded cheddar
    cheese
Salt and pepper to taste

Prepare macaroni and cheese according to package directions. Meanwhile, in a large skillet, brown the turkey or beef with the onion; drain. Stir in vegetables, ketchup, water, mustard and garlic powder. Cook until vegetables are crisp-tender, about 10 minutes. Add cheddar cheese and stir until melted. Mix in macaroni and cheese. Season with salt and pepper. **Yield:** 4-6 servings.

FRUIT FOOL

  1 can (21 ounces) peach *or*
    apricot pie filling
  2 cups whipped topping
1/2 cup flaked coconut, toasted,
    optional
Fresh mint leaves, optional

Combine the pie filling and whipped topping. Spoon into individual dessert dishes. If desired, sprinkle each with coconut and/or garnish with mint. **Yield:** 4-6 servings.

'Eggs-actly' What You Need

BETWEEN her full-time library job at the local high school and the many church and other activities that she's involved in, Amy Lou Strickland of Martinez, Georgia has a hectic schedule. But that's *not* why she sometimes serves this breakfast at suppertime!

"In this part of the country," Amy Lou explains, "we eat breakfast around the clock. My husband's a doctor. Besides being on call for emergencies, he may see patients late in the evening. On nights like those, this quick, delicious meal is a popular standby."

With its half-an-hour preparation time, however, she doesn't limit her No. 1 quick and easy meal to such occasions. "I also enjoy preparing this meal for overnight guests. Plus, when I'm staying with friends, I like to surprise them by fixing it one morning."

At the center of Amy Lou's sunshiny speedy menu is an easy egg dish. "Dinner Eggs is a simple one-dish recipe," she notes. "It's no trouble adapting it to individual tastes, too—for example, for those who like it hot, you can add salsa.

"Quick Blueberry Muffins calls for just a few basic ingredients that don't take much measuring. And the Honey Sauce for Fruit has a refreshing light taste. Pour it over most any fresh fruit —or, in a pinch, even canned fruit—for a fast fruit salad."

No matter which way *she* does it, by the way, Amy Lou has a champion in her corner of the kitchen.

"The Masters Golf Tournament is held near our home," she relates, "and every year I cook for Ben Crenshaw, 1984's winner, his family and friends. This meal's one of his favorites!"

DINNER EGGS

12 slices Canadian bacon
1 package (8 ounces) sliced Swiss cheese
12 eggs
1 pint heavy cream
1/3 cup grated Parmesan cheese
3/4 teaspoon paprika
1/2 teaspoon pepper
2 teaspoons chopped fresh parsley
6 English muffins, split and toasted

Place Canadian bacon in the bottom of a greased 13-in. x 9-in. x 2-in. baking dish; top with Swiss cheese. Break eggs over cheese. Pour cream over eggs and sprinkle with the Parmesan cheese, paprika and pepper. Bake at 400° for 4-8 minutes or until eggs reach desired doneness. Sprinkle with parsley and let stand 5 minutes before serving. Cut between each egg and top each muffin half with an egg, and a slice of bacon and cheese. **Yield:** 6 servings.

QUICK BLUEBERRY MUFFINS

1 cup vanilla ice cream, softened
1 cup self-rising flour
1 cup fresh blueberries
1 tablespoon butter *or* margarine, melted
2 tablespoons sugar

In a medium bowl, mix ice cream and flour. Fold in blueberries. Spoon into six greased muffin cups. Bake at 375° for 20-25 minutes or until muffins test done. While hot, brush muffin tops with butter and sprinkle with sugar. Serve warm. **Yield:** 6 servings.

COME OUT ON TOP. For evenly rounded tops on your muffins, grease muffin cups on the bottom and only 1/2 inch up the sides.

HONEY SAUCE FOR FRUIT

1/4 cup honey
1 cup (8 ounces) sour cream
Fresh fruit

Combine honey and sour cream. Just before serving, drizzle over individual fresh fruit cups. **Yield:** 1-1/4 cups.

A Meal When You're On the Move

WHEN Patty Bryant of Cedar Knolls, New Jersey was organizing a move by her family some years back, she learned all about "labels".

They're not just found on packing cartons, however! For the appetizing evidence of that, you need look no further than the fast and flavorful meal Patty shares here.

"The sauce for my ham dish is one I adapted," she reveals, "from a recipe I spotted on the back of a can of pineapples bits. The combination of pineapple, raisins and seasonings adds a special taste to ordinary ham.

"The topping for the broccoli began on a package of bread crumbs. And my coconut dessert's inspiration came from a can of condensed milk. It's a simple, yet satisfying, bar recipe that bakes in no time."

While this meal's origins may be nothing fancy, you'd never guess it from its inviting appearance. "It's exciting to find dishes that look like they were fussed over when, actually, they took minutes to prepare," Patty relates.

That's especially true these days for this young Eastern wife and mother.

"With a toddler son who's discovering something new every day, I have come to rely on meal plans that are simple," she confirms. "And when I was getting set for our move, I was left even busier."

Don't "label" this meal as merely a time-saver, though. One taste and your family might ask for it even on those rare days when you *do* have a few hours to spare!

HAM WITH PINEAPPLE SAUCE

- 4 slices fully cooked ham (1/2 inch thick)
- 2 tablespoons butter *or* margarine
- 1 can (8 ounces) crushed pineapple, undrained
- 1/2 cup raisins
- 1/4 cup packed brown sugar
- 2 tablespoons prepared mustard
- Dash ground cloves

In a skillet, saute ham slices in butter until warmed. Meanwhile, in a saucepan, combine all of the remaining ingredients; simmer for 3 minutes. Serve over ham. **Yield:** 4 servings.

BROCCOLI SUPREME

- 1 pound fresh broccoli spears
- 1/2 tablespoon butter *or* margarine
- 1/4 cup seasoned bread crumbs
- 1 hard-cooked egg, chopped
- Salt and pepper to taste

Place broccoli and a small amount of water in a saucepan; cover and cook until crisp-tender, about 8-10 minutes. In a small skillet, melt butter. Add bread crumbs and toss to coat. Cook and stir over medium heat until warmed, about 1 minute. Remove from the heat and stir in egg. Drain broccoli; season with salt and pepper. Sprinkle with crumb topping. **Yield:** 4 servings.

LAYERED COCONUT BARS

- 1/4 cup butter *or* margarine, melted
- 1 cup vanilla wafer crumbs
- 1/2 cup semisweet chocolate chips
- 1/4 cup chopped walnuts
- 3/4 cup flaked coconut
- 2/3 cup sweetened condensed milk
- Candied fruit, optional

Combine the butter and crumbs in an 8-in. square baking dish; press down to form a crust. Sprinkle with chocolate chips, walnuts and coconut. Pour milk over all. Bake at 350° for 25 minutes. Decorate with the candied fruit if desired. **Yield:** 9 servings.

Fresh and Flavorful Fare

THERE MUST BE times when Linda Graber of Archbold, Ohio thinks she does her cooking in a school cafeteria instead of a country kitchen.

She arrives home from picking up teenage son Brad at 3:45 p.m....at 5:30, husband Mark's on his way to night-school classes—and, in between, Linda has to feed them and their 6-year-old daughter, Claire, a good nutritious meal!

"With our schedule, I'm often looking for quick, new dishes," Linda says. "But this fast and flavorful meal is one that I rely on regularly.

"The recipe for Chicken Bundles was given to me several years ago by a friend. It's become a family-favorite meal I make often during the week... and during our busy weekends."

Chicken Bundles both go together and cook up fast. "I like the size of the bundles besides," Linda notes. "One is often enough for a young child, while two satisfy adult appetites.

"I adapted my Dilly Cucumber dish from a recipe in a cookbook—I'm always happy to come across a tasty new way to use all of the cucumbers we grow in our vegetable garden.

"The Sugar 'n' Spice Fruit Cups have been a much-requested dessert in my family for years. It goes over big with cinnamon fans!"

Linda's menu zips from start to table in just 30 minutes or less. That's just the half of it, however. "It's great to make a fast dish that also tastes so *good*," she affirms.

Why not try it yourself today...and see if it makes the grade with your gang, too?

CHICKEN BUNDLES

    1 package (8 ounces) cream
      cheese, softened
1/4 cup milk
    1 teaspoon dill weed
1/2 teaspoon salt
1/2 teaspoon pepper
    4 cups cubed cooked chicken
1/2 cup finely chopped celery
    4 green onions with tops,
      thinly sliced
    3 tubes (8 ounces *each*)
      refrigerated crescent rolls
1/4 cup butter *or* margarine,
      melted
1/4 cup seasoned bread crumbs

In a mixing bowl, beat cream cheese, milk, dill, salt and pepper until smooth. Stir in chicken, celery and onions. Unroll crescent roll dough and separate into 12 rectangles, four from each tube; place on a greased baking sheet and press the perforations together. Spoon 1/3 cup of chicken mixture into the center of each rectangle. Bring edges up to the center and pinch to seal. Brush with butter; sprinkle with bread crumbs. Bake at 350° for 15-20 minutes or until golden. **Yield:** 6 servings.

DILLY CUCUMBERS

1/4 cup vinegar
    2 tablespoons vegetable oil
1/4 cup minced fresh dill
      or 1 tablespoon dill weed
    1 teaspoon sugar
    3 to 4 small cucumbers,
      peeled and sliced

In a bowl, combine vinegar, oil, dill and sugar. Add cucumbers and stir well. Refrigerate until serving. **Yield:** 6 servings.

SUGAR 'N' SPICE FRUIT CUP

    4 cups cantaloupe chunks
    3 cups strawberry halves
    3 tablespoons sugar
1/8 teaspoon ground cinnamon

Place fruit in serving bowl. Combine the sugar and cinnamon; sprinkle over fruit and toss gently. Refrigerate until serving. **Yield:** 6 servings.

Skillet Supper Sure to Satisfy

SLOWING DOWN? That's not something Doris Sokolotosky of Smoky Lake, Alberta is likely to set her sights on anytime soon—even though she definitely qualifies as a senior citizen!

"Up until I was 85," this energetic widow comments, "I lived out in the country. And I still appreciate time-saving recipes. I serve on the board of our town museum plus I'm active with other historical work that allows me to attend functions all over the province."

The "30-minutes-or-under-wonder" Doris shares here goes back to when her children (she has three daughters and a son) were university students.

"They'd come home for the weekend and bring along friends," she recalls. "So I needed a meal that was both fast and filling.

"With its slightly tangy sauce, Sweet-and-Sour Pork proved to be the perfect main course. It's a hearty stir-fry, yet it's light enough to leave room for a side dish and dessert.

"For the side dish, I used barbecue sauce to 'pep up' ordinary canned corn. Everyone is always delighted when they sample this variation for the first time.

"Then, one Halloween, I added refreshing Creamwiches for a different type of dessert. They made a 'cool' complement to the other 'hot' dishes in this wonderful meal."

These days, Doris' children are all grown with youngsters of their own. This speedy meal remains a family favorite, however.

"In fact," she reports, "just the other day, I made it for a houseful when a daughter visited from New Zealand. I hosted 17 people in all here."

You don't need to wait for a crowd, though—surprise your family with this tasty treat *today*...and enjoy a bit of extra time out of the kitchen yourself.

CREAMWICHES

8 frozen waffles
1/3 cup orange marmalade
2 tablespoons chopped pecans

1 pint vanilla ice cream
Additional marmalade and chopped pecans, optional

Toast waffles; cool. In a small bowl, mix marmalade and nuts. Spread over one side of waffles. Cut ice cream into four slices; sandwich one slice between two waffles, with marmalade toward inside. Top with additional marmalade and pecans if desired. **Yield:** 4 servings.

HELPFUL HONEY TIP. Always store honey at room temperature. Refrigeration speeds up crystallization.

TANGY CORN

1 can (15 to 16 ounces) whole kernel corn, drained
1 can (15 ounces) cream-style corn
3 tablespoons bottled barbecue sauce

Combine all ingredients in a saucepan; cook over medium heat for 5 minutes or until heated through. **Yield:** 4-6 servings.

SWEET-AND-SOUR PORK

1 can (20 ounces) pineapple chunks
2 tablespoons cornstarch
1/4 cup soy sauce
1 tablespoon honey
1/2 teaspoon instant chicken bouillon granules
1 garlic clove, minced
1/8 teaspoon pepper
2 tablespoons cooking oil
3/4 pound pork tenderloin, cut into bite-size pieces
1 medium green pepper, thinly sliced
Hot rice

Drain pineapple, reserving the juice; set pineapple aside. Add enough water to juice to equal 3/4 cup. Add cornstarch, soy sauce, honey, bouillon, garlic and pepper; set aside. Heat oil in a large skillet; cook and stir pork and green pepper for 6-8 minutes or until pork is no longer pink and green pepper is crisp-tender. Stir pineapple juice mixture into skillet with pineapple. Cook until thickened and bubbly. Serve over rice. **Yield:** 4 servings.

INDEX